The Illustrated
Wordsworth's Guide
To The Lakes

A view of Derwentwater in 1809, watercolour signed J. G.
(probably Joshua Green). The western shore of the lake.

THE ILLUSTRATED
WORDSWORTH'S GUIDE
TO THE LAKES

EDITED BY PETER BICKNELL

Foreword by Alan G. Hill
Professor of English, Royal Holloway College,
University of London

CONGDON & WEED, INC.

NEW YORK

For Ellen, who has given me a home from home
in the District of the Lakes

This edition copyright © Webb & Bower (Publishers) Limited 1984
Introduction copyright © Peter Bicknell 1984

A Webb & Bower Book
Edited, designed and produced by
Webb & Bower (Publishers) Limited
Exeter, England

Library of Congress Cataloging in Publication Data
Wordsworth, William, 1770–1850.
The illustrated Wordsworth's guide to the lakes.

Rev. ed. of: A guide through the district of the
lakes in the north of England.
1. Lake District (England)—Description and travel—
Guide-books. I. Bicknell, Peter. II. Title.
III. Guide through the district of the lakes in the
north of England.
DA670.L1W67 1984   914.27′8   83–23176
ISBN 0–86553–114–5
ISBN 0–312–92326–0 (St. Martin's Press)

Published by Congdon & Weed, Inc.
298 Fifth Avenue, New York, N.Y. 10001
Distributed by St. Martin's Press
175 Fifth Avenue, New York, N.Y. 10010

First published in Great Britain 1984 by
Webb & Bower (Publishers) Limited

All Rights Reserved
Typeset in Great Britain
Printed and bound in Hong Kong
First American Edition

CONTENTS

Foreword

The painter's eye and the poet's vision are often directed to similar ends. Nowadays, literary critics and art historians are much more conscious of the ways in which visual image and printed word can illuminate each other. No clearer focus could be found for demonstrating this than Romantic landscape, and no more relevant text than Wordsworth's *Guide to the Lakes*.

It is now almost impossible to conjure up the Lake District which Wordsworth knew and delineated with such precision and power in this little prose work. But with the help of the artists who recorded it in such variety and profusion before and during his lifetime (and often indeed under his inspiration and guidance), the reader and visitor of today can recapture something of the freshness and mystery that excited the early tourists for whom the poet was writing.

Peter Bicknell needs no introduction to those who know him as a writer on topography and illustration, and for the pioneering exhibitions he has arranged at Cambridge and Grasmere. He has made a special study of the artists and writers who 'discovered' the Lakes in search of the picturesque and sublime, and he brings his own unrivalled expertise and flair, as well as an intimate knowledge of the region itself, to the preparation of this, the first fully-illustrated edition of Wordsworth's *Guide*. Taken together, text and plates build up a unique portrait of the milieu in which the Lake Poets lived and wrote. They also go a long way towards explaining why the Lake District has continued to cast such a potent spell over the English imagination up to the present day.

Wordsworth's *Guide*, a classic of its kind, is not as widely known as it deserves to be, and I am very happy to have this opportunity of commending this new edition which offers so many fresh insights into his central concerns. Wordsworth was a great visionary poet; and yet the *Guide* was not the work of a dreamer or recluse but a practical countryman who lived out his principles among his native mountains and lakes. He wished ordinary people to understand the landscapes and the time-honoured lifestyle which had nurtured his deepest intuitions about Man and Nature and the 'Truth that cherishes our daily life.' Never before, or indeed since, has a humble guidebook served such a lofty purpose.

ALAN G. HILL

Introduction

William Wordsworth was born on 7th April, 1770, on the fringe of the Lake District at Cockermouth, within sight of the summit of Skiddaw and only five miles from Bassenthwaite Lake. Apart from a brief period the Lake District was his home for the eighty years of his life. His last fifty were spent continuously at Grasmere and Rydal. His 'dear native regions', the places that he knew so intimately and loved so well, were one of the main sources of inspiration for his poetry; so it is not surprising that they also inspired his most popular prose work, the work which became in the fifth edition in 1835 *A Guide Through the District of the Lakes*. When the second version was published in 1820, annexed to *The River Duddon Sonnets*, he explained in an introductory note that it was written 'in the same spirit which dictated several of the poems, and from a belief that it will tend naturally to illustrate them'. Wordsworth's view of nature was revolutionary, and, whether we agree with him or not, he has fundamentally changed the way we all look at the natural world. He conceived of nature as herself endowed with life and powers beyond the human scale. (In the 'Description of the Scenery of the Lakes' in the *Guide* the word 'Nature', spelt with a capital N, occurs thirty-eight times). The life of nature and the life of man were inextricably bound up in each other. It was the creative and contemplative powers of the individual mind which enabled man to achieve a balanced relationship with the 'goodly universe'.

Wordsworth's highly personal view of nature crystalized in the few years when, at Racedown and Alfoxden, in the West Country, his relationship with Coleridge was at its closest. Together they were creating *Lyrical Ballads*, and together they saw eye to eye. As Coleridge wrote in *Biographica Literaria*, 1817:

The two cardinal points of poetry, the power of exciting the sympathy of the reader by a faithful adherence to the truth of nature, and the power of giving the interests of novelty by the modifying colours of imagination. The sudden charm which accidents of light and shade, which moonlight or sunset diffused over a known and familiar landscape, appeared to represent the practicability of combining both. These are the poetry of nature.

Cockermouth by Joseph Farington, looking towards the northern fells of the
Lake District. Wordsworth was, he said, 'much favour'd in his birthplace', a
substantial house of 1745, in the main street of Cockermouth, with a garden
running down to the River Derwent. The house belonged to Sir James Lowther,
by whom his father was employed as agent. The letter press for Farington's first
book of views of the Lakes, published in 1789, was probably written by
Wordsworth's uncle, William Cookson.

They are also the two cardinal points of the *Guide*, though it is 'adherence to the truth of nature' which gets by far the greater emphasis.

Mathew Arnold's much quoted story of the well meaning parson who, after congratulating Wordsworth on the success of the *Guide*, asked him if he had written anything else, is probably apocryphal; yet it is significant comment on the popularity of the book. Today the situation is reversed when it comes as a surprise to many, familiar with Wordsworth the poet, to discover that he wrote a guide to the Lake District.

It is often assumed, quite incorrectly, that Wordsworth and the 'Lake Poets' were responsible for the 'discovery' of the Lakes. By the time Wordsworth had embarked on writing the *Guide*, the dons, the divines and the draughtsmen had been making the tour of the Lakes for fifty years—the Lake District was already established as a fashionable resort. It was a more popular subject for description and illustration than any other region in the British Isles. More than thirty accounts of tours had been published as well as several handsome volumes of views. It was a Mecca for landscape artists— Gainsborough, de Loutherbourg, Towne, Turner and Constable were among those who had made tours. Smith's *New and Accurate Map of the Lakes*, intended for tourists, was in general use, and was advertised in West's *Guide* which itself was in its ninth edition. Plumptre had written *The Lakers*, a comic opera satirizing the tourists. And the gentleman artists and writers had already begun to form colonies at Ambleside and Grasmere.

Until the middle of the eighteenth century the mountains and lakes formed an unprofitable wilderness of little interest to any one but those who had to extract a living from it. Daniel Defoe, writing in the 1720s, found 'Westmoreland, a country being eminent only for being the wildest, most barren and frightful of any that I have passed over in England or even in Wales itself'. To Celia Fiennes, in 1698, potted char and the making of clap bread were of far more interest than the scenery. It was not till the 1750s that the first visitors came to the Lakes specifically to enjoy the scenery. Two artists, William Bellers and Thomas Smith of Derby were there soon after 1750. Bellers' first print of Derwentwater in 1752 and Smith's of a similar view in 1761, both published in London, brought the beauties of the lakes and mountains to the metropolis. The first of the writers were the Rev. John Dalton of Queen's College, Oxford, and the Rev. Dr John Brown of St John's College, Cambridge, both Cumbrian by birth, who visited Keswick in about 1753 and described the beauties of the landscape in picturesque terms, Dalton in a poem addressed to the Misses Lowther, and Brown in a letter, which also included a poem, addressed to Lord Lyttelton. These visitors belonged to a generation of English gentlemen who were learning to appreciate the beauties of natural scenery, but only if it conformed with the landscapes of the painters working in Italy in the seventeenth century. Many of these gentlemen, in making the Grand Tour, had become familiar with the paintings of these artists and the scenes that had inspired them—the Virgilian tranquillity of the Campagna evoked by Claude Lorrain, and the horror of Alp and Apennine evoked by Salvator Rosa. When they began to visit the wilder parts of their native land they viewed the prospect of lake and mountain, precipice and cataract, as a series of pictures. The early artists in

A View of Derwentwater, towards Borrodale by William Bellers . . . October 10, 1752. This is the earliest print of British mountain scenery to adopt the picturesque conventions derived from the seventeenth-century landscape painters such as Claude, Salvator, and Poussin. Bellers' prints brought the beauties of the Lakes to the metropolis.

the Lakes converted what they saw into 'Italian' compositions, and the writers described what they saw in terms of pictures. Dr John Brown explained that

the full perfection of KESWICK consist of three circumstances, *Beauty, Horror,* and *Immensity* united . . .   But to give you a complete idea of these three perfections, as they are joined in KESWICK, would require the united powers of Claude, Salvator, and Poussin.*

* In England in the eighteenth century when 'Poussin' was referred to, it was generally to Gaspard Dughet, 1615–75 and not to his now better known brother-in-law Nicolas Poussin 1594–1665.

Dr Brown sets the picturesque pattern for Lake District tourists for the next fifty years. The innumerable Tours and Descriptions that came out in this period invariably treat the scenery as a series of prospects to be described as pictures. Most of these books, which rely for colour on quoting each other's purple passages, are of little literary merit. An exception is the poet Thomas

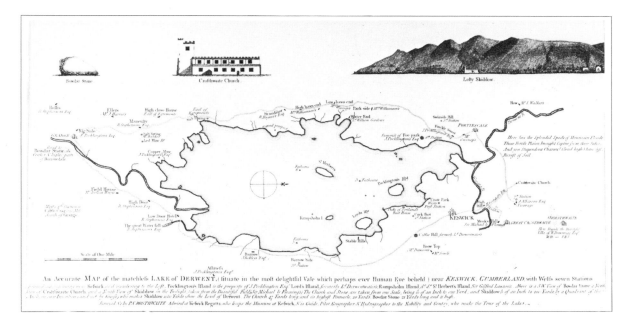

'An Accurate Map of the matchless Lake of Derwent, (situate in the most delightful Vale which perhaps ever Human Eye beheld). Surveyed etc. by P. Crosthwaite Admiral at Keswick Regatta; who keeps the Museum at Keswick, & is Guide, Pilot, Geographer & Hydrographer to the Nobility and Gentry, who make the Tour of the Lakes. Published and sold by Peter Crosthwaite, the Author, at his Museum Keswick. August 20th, 1784', showing West's eight Stations.

Gray's journal of his tour in the autumn of 1769, when he spent six days at Keswick 'lap'd in Elysium'. It is a sensitive and unpretentious record, commended by Wordsworth for its 'distinctness and unaffected simplicity'. In observations such as, 'Saddleback, whose furrowed sides were gilt by the noon-day sun, whilst its brow appeared of a sad purple, from the shadow of the clouds as they sailed slowly by', there is a hint of Wordsworth and the romantic association of mood with landscape. And for Wordsworth Gray's description of the view of Grasmere from Dunmail Raise, 'one of the sweetest landscapes that art ever attempted to imitate', had a special appeal. 'Not a single red tile, no gentleman's flaring house, or garden walls, break in upon this little unsuspected paradise; but all is peace, rusticity, and happy poverty, in its neatest, most becoming attire.' However Gray was not above making the best of the sublime Salvatorial aspects of places like Gowdar Crag at the entrance to Borrowdale, where 'the rocks ... hanging loose and nodding forwards, seem just starting from their base in shivers ... the place reminds me of those passes in the Alps, where the guides tell you to move with speed, and say nothing, lest the agitation of the air should loosen the snow above, and bring down a mass that would overwhelm a caravan.'

The high priest of the Picturesque was the Cumbrian born Rev. William Gilpin. He invented the term 'Picturesque Beauty', which he defined as 'that which would look well in a picture'. His book *Observations Relative Chiefly to Picturesque Beauty made in the Year 1772 on ... the Mountains and Lakes of Cumberland, and Westmoreland* is not so much a journal of a tour or a guide for tourists as instructions on how they should view the landscape. Gilpin was the first author to enter the controversial field of the aesthetics of the Picturesque, and his book is full of picturesque theory. His illustrations, based on his own sketches, are not as he points out intended to be topographical portraits, but picturesque arrangements of the elements in a view. Nature, for all her beauties, was unequal in composition; so Gilpin often had to put things right for her. Wordsworth was familiar with the works of Gilpin, and frequently found himself in agreement, as, for instance, over the dictum that 'white destroys the *gradation* of distance; and, therefore, an object of pure white can scarcely ever be managed with good effect in landscape painting'.

The first guide book to the Lakes appeared in 1778. This was *A Guide to the Lakes: dedicated to the Lovers of Landscape Studies and to all who have Visited or intend to Visit the Lakes ...* written anonymously by a Jesuit priest, Thomas West. He was primarily an antiquarian, but as indicated in the title of his *Guide*, landscape was not only an object of love, but also of study, and the study is picturesque. He plans the tour so that 'the change of scenes is from what is pleasing, to what is surprising, from the delicate and elegant touches of Claude to the noble scenes of Poussin, and from these to the stupendous romantic ideas of Salvator Rosa'. The design of the book is to 'encourage the taste of visiting the Lakes by furnishing the traveller with a Guide; and for that purpose are here collected and laid before him, all the select stations, and points of view noticed by those who have made the tour of the lakes'. These stations are enumerated and described in the text. They are shown on the Plans of the Lakes, surveyed and first published in 1783 by Peter Crosthwaite who described himself as 'Admiral at Keswick Regatta; who keeps the Museum at Keswick, & is Guide, Pilot, Geographer & Hydrographer to the Nobility and Gentry who make the Tour of the Lakes'. West's Guide, extensively revised and augmented by William Cockin in 1780, was in general use for half a century; its first real rivals being the first separate edition of Wordsworth's in 1822 and Otley's in 1823. The last edition of West's was published in 1821. Wordsworth makes several references to Mr West, 'whose Guide to the Lakes has been eminently serviceable to the Tourist for nearly fifty years'. As a boy Wordsworth had been delighted by the view from the 'station' above the ferry house on the west bank of Windermere, the site of which 'was long ago pointed out by Mr West in his Guide as the pride of the Lakes'. West advocates the use of the

Pencil study of a man sketching, using a Claude glass, by Gainsborough
c. 1750–55. Although Wordsworth would not have approved of the picturesque
formalizing of Nature in a Claude glass, they were still in general use during his
life. When in 1805 the skeleton of Charles Gough, whose misfortune on
Helvellyn inspired Wordsworth's poem 'Fidelity', was found, there was a
Claude glass in his pocket.

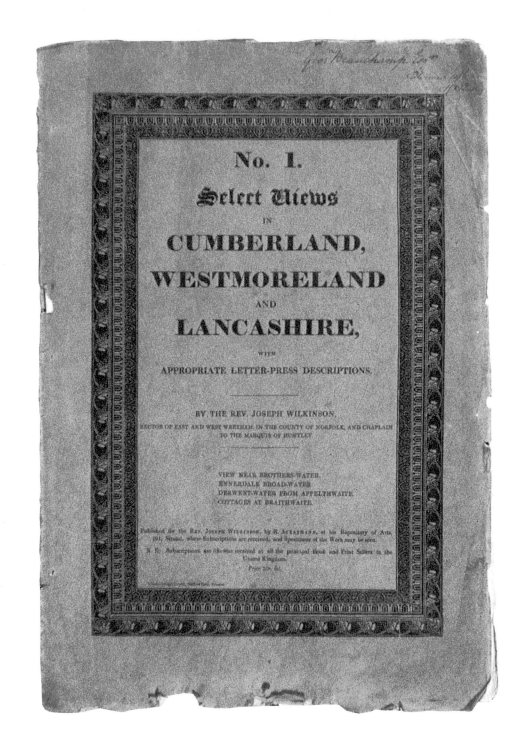

No. 1.

Select Views

IN

CUMBERLAND,

WESTMORELAND

AND

LANCASHIRE,

WITH

APPROPRIATE LETTER-PRESS DESCRIPTIONS.

BY THE REV. JOSEPH WILKINSON,

RECTOR OF EAST AND WEST WRETHAM, IN THE COUNTY OF NORFOLK, AND CHAPLAIN
TO THE MARQUIS OF HUNTLEY.

VIEW NEAR BROTHERS-WATER.
ENNERDALE BROAD-WATER.
DERWENT-WATER FROM APPLETHWAITE.
COTTAGES AT BRAITHWAITE.

Published for the Rev. Joseph Wilkinson, by R. Ackermann, at his Repository of Arts,
101, Strand, where Subscriptions are received, and Specimens of the Work may be seen.

N. B. Subscriptions are likewise received at all the principal Book and Print Sellers in the
United Kingdom.

Price 10s. 6d.

14

landscape mirror, which had become an essential article of equipment for every 'Laker'. This device, generally known as a Claude Glass, consisted of a small tinted convex mirror, in which, rather like the viewfinder of a camera, the tourist could see the prospect condensed and framed, and suffused with the mellow glow of Claude's visions of Elysium. Nothing epitomizes the Picturesque better than the use of these glasses. The viewer literally turned his back on the actual landscape to see its image as a picture in a frame.

By the time Wordsworth was at work on the *Guide*, the picturesque tour had become a subject for satire. The Rev. James Plumptre, of Clare College Cambridge, made tours in 1796, 1797 and 1799. As well as being an academic divine of literary tastes he was a keen amateur of the theatre and of opera. A typical 'Laker' himself, he wrote after his second tour a comic opera (published but never known to have been performed) entitled *The Lakers*, in which the principal characters indulge in the more extravagant affectations of the Picturesque. Miss Beccabunga Veronique is a keen botanist, sketcher and writer of Gothic novels. 'Give me my glasses', she cries. 'Where's my Gray? Oh! Claude– and Poussin are nothing. By the Bye, where's my Claude Lorrain? I must throw a Gilpin tint over these magic scenes of beauty.' And it is a caricature of the Rev. William Gilpin which began to appear in 1809 as the hero of Combe and Rowlandson's *The Tour of Doctor Syntax in Search of the Picturesque*. Before setting out on his tour Syntax declares:

> I'll make a TOUR—and then I'll WRITE IT
> You well know what my pen can do,
> I'll prove it with my pencil too:—
> I'll ride and write and sketch and print,
> And thus create a real mint;
> I'll prose it here, I'll prose it there.
> I'll picturesque it ev'ry where.

The alternative title was Doctor Syntax's Tour to the Lakes; and the climax of the tour was, as it had been for Gray and many others, when he reached the Lake of Keswick.

Wordsworth's Guide differed fundamentally from any of the previous literature of the Lakes. His predecessors, with the exception of West, had written after a somewhat cursory acquaintance with the district—some of

Opposite: The first appearance of the *Guide*. The front wrapper of the original monthly part published Jan 1 1810 of Wilkinson's *Select Views*. It contained the dedication, four pages of the introduction and eight plates.

them after a visit of only a few days. Wordsworth's writing was based on a profound and intimate knowledge of the country and the people who lived in it. 'My book,' he said, 'could not have been written without much experience.' The 'Lakers' did not depart from well worn tracks, and viewed nature from prescribed stations. Wordsworth wandered freely over a countryside which he perceived, not as convention demanded he should, but as he actually saw it. Although he frequently adopted the vocabulary of the Picturesque, and when young was considerably influenced by the writings of Gray, Gilpin, West and the others, he reacted against 'liking, by rules of mimic art transferr'd/To things above all art'. For this as he explains in *The Prelude*:

> Although a strong infection of the age,
> Was never much my habit, giving way
> To a comparison of scene with scene,
> Bent over much on superficial things,
> Pampering myself with meagre novelties
> Of colour and proportion, to the moods
> Of time and season, to the moral power
> The affections, and the spirit of the place,
> Less sensible.

The quintessence of the message which he wished to convey to his readers is in these lines. As de Selincourt has succinctly put it, 'there are few pages of the *Guide to the Lakes* which fail to record the poet'. The prose throughout is vitalized by the personal devotion and the same response to nature that informs the poetry. Passages like that which begins, 'Not a breath of air, no restlessness of insects and not a moving object perceptible—except the clouds gliding in the depths of the lake' are as true an interpretation of the 'poetry of nature' as many of the finest passages in *The Prelude*.

The work, which for the last half of the poet's life was never far from his mind, seems already to have been started in August 1807, when he told Lady Holland that he was 'preparing a manual to guide travellers in their tour amongst the Lakes'. However, a year later in answer to a request by the Rev. J. Pering, he was refusing to write a description of the scenery, with 'an apology for not venturing on a theme so boundless as this sublime and beautiful region'. 'Objects,' he said, 'may be too familiar to a Man, to leave him the power of describing them. This is the case with me in regard to these Lakes and mountains, which are my native Country among which I have passed the greatest part of my life.' So it seems inconsistent that only two years later he agreed to write the descriptive text for a volume of views of the Lakes.

The *Guide* made its first appearance in 1810 as an anonymous introduction to the Rev. Joseph Wilkinson's *Select Views in Cumberland, Westmoreland, and Lancashire*. Wilkinson had lived at Ormathwaite, on the western slope below Skiddaw a few miles from Keswick, until he moved to Norfolk in 1804. He was a friend of the Coleridges and the Southeys at Greta Hall and an acquaintance of the Wordsworths. He was a conscientious but not very talented amateur artist. His views were reproduced as forty-eight large soft-

Penrith, watercolour by
Peter de Wint. Penrith, five
miles from the foot of
Ullswater, was the home
town of both Wordsworth's
parents. In 1776–7
Wordsworth, his sister
Dorothy and his future wife
Mary Hutchinson, attended
Ann Birkett's infant school at
Penrith, staying with their
Cookson grandparents.

Skiddaw by William Westall. Keswick is seen as it was in 1820, eighteen years
before the church of St John the Evangelist, with its prominent spire, had been
built. Crosthwaite church can be seen in the distance, with a glimpse of
Bassenthwaite beyond. The ascent of Skiddaw, the fourth highest summit in the
Lakes, had been a standard expedition for the more adventurous tourist since the
1750s. The ascent could be made on a pony.

Town End, Grasmere, watercolour by Thomas Miles Richardson. The group of houses was on the old main road to Ambleside, south of the village of Grasmere, which included the Wordsworths' cottage. It was once a pub, the Dove and Olive Branch, and only became 'Dove Cottage' long after the Wordsworths lived there. The new main road by the side of the lake, which Wordsworth regretted, was opened in 1836.

Bowness on Windermere rearranged by Thomas Walmesly, 1808. This view from the ferry has been romanticized to form a picture little related to the actual landscape. The tower is either Bowness church moved more than half a mile to the south or the castellated 'station' transported from the other side of the lake. The Salvatorian precipice is pure invention, and Belle Isle and the circular house have been moved and transformed. This picturesque departure from actuality is the antithesis of Wordsworth's 'faithful adherence to the truth of Nature'.

Curwen Island on Windermere from the Station, by William Green. 'The site was long ago pointed out by Mr West in his Guide, as the pride of the lakes, and now goes by the name of "The Station". So much used I to be delighted with the view from it, while a little boy, that ... I led thither from Hawkshead a youngster about my own age, an Irish boy, who was a servant to an itinerant conjurer. My motive was to witness the pleasure I expected the boy would receive from the prospect of the islands below and the intermingling water. I was not disappointed.'

The title page of *Southey's Poetical Works*, 1845, with a vignette of 'Mr. Southey's residence at Keswick', by his wife Caroline. Coleridge rented half of Greta Hall, a handsome house on a knoll near the bridge over the Greta in Keswick, which he occupied with his wife Sara (née Fricker) and his son Hartley in the summer of 1800. Three years later they were joined by Southey and his wife, Sara's sister Caroline. Greta Hall is thirteen miles from Dove Cottage. There were frequent exchanges of visits between the two households, and meetings at the half-way point on the banks of Thirlmere.

A plate from *Select Views*.
View in St John's Vale with Greencrag.
Typical of Wilkinson's amateurish draughtsmanship
of which Wordsworth was so critical.

ground etchings by W. F. Wells, a highly skilled professional engraver, who faithfully reproduced the deficiencies of Wilkinson's drawings. That Wordsworth was conscious of these deficiencies is evident from a letter to Lady Beaumont, 10th May 1810:

The drawings, or etchings, or whatever they may be called, are, I know, such as to you and Sir George must be intolerable. You will receive from them that sort of disgust which I do from bad poetry, a disgust which can never be felt in its full strength but by those who are practised in an art, as well as amateurs of it ... I do, however, sincerely hope that the author and his wife ... may be spared the mortification of having them condemned severely by acknowledged judges. They will please many who in all the arts are most taken by what is most worthless.

Hard words, which explain why Wordsworth did not wish his name to be associated with the book. Loyalty to a friend and perhaps a desperate need of an author's fee seem to have overcome any scruples about contributing, so long as his anonymity was preserved.

Select Views came out serially in twelve monthly parts. Wordsworth was still writing the end of his introduction before the last of the parts had been issued; and he was already planning a guide on his own, which Dorothy thought 'would be likely to bring him more money than any of his higher labours'. The second version of the *Guide* appeared in 1820 as *A Topographical Description of the Country of the Lakes in the North of England*, annexed to *The River Duddon, a Series of Sonnets : and other Poems*.

The *Topographical Description* had a good press, and its success encouraged Wordsworth to publish in 1822 *A Description of the Scenery of the Lakes in the North of England*, as a separate volume of a handy size to carry in the pocket. It was again extensively revised, included a map, and among the additions was an unacknowledged version of Dorothy Wordsworth's account of her excursion up Scawfell Pike. As only 500 copies were printed, another edition was soon needed. The fourth edition which was published in 1823, with the same title as the previous one, included further additions, notably accounts of Dorothy's 'Excursions to the Top of Scawfell and on the Banks of Ullswater' which now formed a separate section.

Wordsworth's final version, the one which is reproduced in this volume, was published in 1835 by Hudson and Nicholson of Kendal as *A Guide through the District of the Lakes* ... In this form it differs considerably from the original *Select Views*, but it remains essentially the same book. Wordsworth's appreciation of the district had changed little in twenty-five years.

After this, the fifth edition, the book was taken over by Hudson and Nicholson who republished it in 1842 as part of a more comprehensive *Complete Guide* under their own editorship. Wordsworth continued to take an active interest; he read proofs, helped to persuade Professor Sedgwick to contribute three letters on geology, recommended that Thomas Gough of Kendal should supply botanical lists, suggested that De Quincey or Hartley Coleridge should check Nicholson's glossary of place names, and received remuneration from the publishers. Hudson's *Guide* was published twice more in Wordsworth's life time, in 1843 and 1846. Each time the technical information which had become an essential part of a tourist's guide was augmented.

Among several reprints of the 1835 edition, three are of special interest. In 1906 the great Wordsworth scholar, Ernest de Selincourt, edited it with an introduction, appendices, textual and illustrative notes, a map and eight plates. His introduction covered the history of the *Guide* and of its literary antecedents, together with much critical comment. His informative notes clarify in some detail the differences between Wordsworth's five editions. W. M. Merchant, in his introduction to a 1951 reprint, covers much of the same ground as de Selincourt, dealing in particular with the Picturesque and its influence on Wordsworth. W. J. B. Owen and Jane Worthington Smyser, in their monumental *Prose Works of William Wordsworth*, 1974, reprinted the 1835 edition with a profusion of scholarly comment and annotation, including many important references to and quotations from related manuscripts. They analyse in great detail Wordsworth's sources and the changes in his text. The main changes from edition to edition are covered by the Bibliographical Note at the end of this volume.

In writing the *Guide* Wordsworth relied on the help of the ladies of the household. All three, Dorothy, Mary and Sara Hutchinson, acted as scribes, most of the manuscript material being in Mary's hand. Dorothy actually wrote some of the descriptive passages. On 12th November, 1810, she recorded, 'In the evening Wm. employed me to compose a description or two for the finishing of his work for Wilkinson.' The 'Excursions to the top of Scawfell and on the Banks of Ullswater' are edited versions of Dorothy's recorded accounts. Some of the simple brilliance of her prose has been lost in the editing. Wordsworth's descriptive prose, a minor part of the *Guide* as a whole, seems to owe a considerable debt to the sparkling clarity of Dorothy's.

In its final form as edited by Hudson, the *Guide* accepts the changes which had taken place in the nature of tourism, such as the popular desire for information on scientific subjects like botany and geology. Bradshaw's first Lake District railway timetable had been issued in 1848. Because of their relevance to the last phases of Wordsworth's interest in his *Guide*, his two letters to the Editor of the *Morning Post* in 1884 on the proposed Kendal and Windermere Railway, which include the sonnet 'Is then no nook of English ground secure', are included here as an appendix. They form a sad postscript. His vehement attack on the proposals, which were strongly supported by local interests, brought him a 'torrent of abuse'. The need to preserve the area from the bad taste of the invading gentry had been a concern of particular urgency to the poet, and now he saw a new threat, from another quarter, for 'artisans and labourers, and the humbler classes of shopkeepers should not be tempted to visit particular spots which they had not been educated to appreciate'. Despite Wordsworth, the Windermere Railway was opened on 21st April 1847. It is a nice irony that when recently there were proposals to close the railway, the spiritual descendants of Wordsworth, The Friends of the Lake District, launched a successful campaign to preserve it.

One of those who welcomed the railway was Harriet Martineau. She impinged on the Wordsworth circle in 1845, when at the age of forty-three and already established as a successful writer on political economy, practical

Picnic on Windermere. Pen and ink, and wash drawing by John Harden. The generous entertainment at Brathay Hall frequently included expeditions in boats, and picnics. Many visits were exchanged with the Wordsworths at Grasmere and Rydal.

divinity and social problems, she settled at Ambleside. Though Wordsworth helped her choose a site for her house there was no great sympathy between them. She reacted strongly against the concept of the 'unsuspected paradise', seeing neither the country of the Lakes nor the people who lived there as romantic. Wordsworth's beloved Nature had done her part 'in providing rock for foundations, the purest air, and the amplest supply of running water; yet people live . . . in stench, huddled together in cabins, and almost without water'. Five years after the poet's death she published her *Complete Guide to the Lakes*. In this she conscientiously guided the new urban tourists, supporting her itineraries with a wealth of useful information, maps, outlines of mountains prepared by Mr Flintoft and Mr Ruthven's coloured geological map of the district. She even encouraged the idea of fell walking and of mountain climbing, provided the tourist was accompanied by a guide.

Although, since the death of Wordsworth, there has been a continued interest in the *Guide* and many republications, there has never been a fully illustrated edition. In the original version for *Select Views* the letterpress was ostensibly a description of Wilkinson's plates, which were not illustrations of the text. De Selincourt's six selected views (supplemented by four more in the 1980 reprint) and John Piper's drawings for Merchant's edition which, in the words of the dust jacket, 'throw a fresh light on otherwise familiar scenes and illustrate the timelessness of Wordsworth's narrative', only supplement it to a very limited extent. Wordsworth's book is concerned with the visual image; and in the past the reader has had to rely on his own imagination or his memory of familiar scenes to create the image.

The object of the present volume is to present Wordsworth's final text, enriched by a profusion of visual images created by artists working in his lifetime or by those working earlier, with whose pictures he could have been familiar. These pictures have been supplemented by the publishers with a few photographs taken recently to show aspects of the landscape which remain today much as Wordsworth knew them, or which have been so altered by development, like the damming of Thirlmere and the afforestation of Ennerdale that a landscape has been created which the poet would bitterly have resented.

Although Wordsworth told R. P. Graves, a curate at Windermere, that as well as the callings of poet and landscape gardener he also considered himself fitted for that of 'critic of pictures and works of art', he does not really seem to have been much concerned with these matters. Through his friendship with Sir George Beaumont, the talented amateur artist, key figure and patron in the world of painters, he must have been in touch with what was going on in artistic circles. At Brathay Hall, at the head of Windermere and within easy walking distance of Grasmere, John Harden, another talented amateur, extended his hospitality to many artists. It was here in 1806 that Wordsworth met John Constable, who remarked 'upon the high opinion Wordsworth entertains of Himself'. Much later, through the influence of Sir George and Lady Beaumont, poet and painter developed a notable admiration for each other. With the Beaumonts Wordsworth met the celebrated artists, Haydon and Wilkie, and it seems to have been history, portrait and genre painting, rather than landscape, to which he responded. Some light on Wordsworth's

Robert Southey. Pencil and chalk drawing by Henry Edridge at Keswick in 1814. Coleridge and Southey were the first writers to be linked with Wordsworth as the 'Lake Poets'. This popular term was originally used in a derogatory sense in a review of John Wilson's (Christopher North) *The Isle of Palms and other Poems*, in the *Edinburgh Review* of 1812. 'This is a new recruit to the company of the Lake Poets. Mr Wilson is not free from some of the faults of diction which we think belong to the school.' The idea of a 'School' had been fabricated by Francis Jeffrey in anonymous reviews of works by Southey and Wordsworth in the *Edinburgh Review*, 1802 and 1807. Wordsworth first met Coleridge and Southey in 1795. He was on intimate terms with Coleridge until the estrangements in 1810. Coleridge was only resident in the Lakes during these few years. His principal contribution to Lake District writing is an account of a solitary walking tour in August 1802 (*Inquiring Spirit*, edited by Kathleen Coburn, 1951). Southey followed Coleridge to Keswick and lived there for the rest of his life. Although he frequently met Wordsworth they were little in sympathy with each other. Neither Coleridge nor Southey made any contribution to Wordsworth's *Guide*.

Rydal Mount in 1831, watercolour by William Westall.
This sketch which is in Dora Wordsworth's album was drawn at a time when
Westall was a frequent visitor at Rydal Mount.

lack of any enthusiastic response to landscape painting is shed by a note to his poem 'Descriptive Sketches' in which he says of the Alps, 'Whoever in attempting to describe their sublime features, should confine himself to the cold rules of painting would give his reader but a very imperfect idea of those emotions which they have the irresistible power of communicating to the most impassive imaginations. The fact is, that controlling influence, which distinguishes the Alps from all other scenery, is derived from images which disdain the pencil.' Crabb Robinson in 1835 recorded that 'Wordsworth did not spare even Turner when he was condemning other modern painters'. He was, no doubt, influenced by Sir George Beaumont who continually attacked Turner. Wordsworth may well have felt that Turner often overstepped the mark in investing a scene with greater emotional significance than it could support. He probably also reacted against Turner's and even Constable's 'modernism'.

The only reference to an English painter in the *Guide* occurs when the author, in describing the approaches to the Lake District, recommends a visit to Hardraw Scar in Wensleydale, 'of which with its waterfall, Turner has a fine drawing'. William Westall, a faithful interpreter of Lakeland landscape, was one of the few artists to be closely associated with the Wordsworth circle. He was a warm friend of Southey, and provided illustrations of Lake scenes for some of his books. Southey provided, gratis, the letterpress for Westall's *Lake and Vale of Keswick* Westall stayed at Rydal Mount when he was preparing his panoramic views of the Lakes, Wordsworth helping him with the place names to be engraved on the plates. At that time he was also working on illustrations for an edition of Wordsworth's works, some of which were published without any text.

In writing about the Lakes Wordsworth was not influenced by the work of the landscape painters in the way he was by the Picturesque writers. There are however exceptions in his verse. Three sonnets were 'Suggested by Mr Westall's Views of the Caves etc. in Yorkshire'; and the 'Elegiac Stanzas', inspired by the death of his brother John in the wreck of his ship *The Earl of Abergavenny*, responded to Sir George Beaumont's painting 'Peel Castle', showing ships in peril on the sea. Many visions of lake and mountain by Turner and others are every bit as imaginative as those of Wordsworth. As romantic interpretations of nature they are parallel expressions. They owe nothing directly to the poet, nor does the poet owe anything to them.

Many of the illustrations in this volume reproduce plates from Lake District books, rather than the original works of the artists. At a time when there were few public galleries, no photographic reproductions of pictures, and travel was slow and laborious, Wordsworth would have been much more familiar with prints than with the paintings and drawings themselves. He was well acquainted with the prints of Farington, Green and Westall, artists whose aim was to record the district with topographical accuracy; so their views show us the scene, not only as Wordsworth knew it, but presented in a way which was familiar to him. His copy of Rose's *Westmorland, Cumberland etc. Illustrated*, which covered every corner of the district with a profusion of engravings from drawings by Allom, Pickering and Gastineau, is still in the Wordsworth family.

Three views by James Baker Pyne, showing the tourists established in the
Lakes. Pyne was commissioned by Thomas Agnew of Manchester to make a
series of paintings of the Lakes, twenty-five of which were published as
lithographs in 1853. Although this is three years after Wordsworth's death the
original sketches had been done earlier, and show the Lakes as they were at the
end of Wordsworth's life. *Above*: Lake Windermere Regatta. The scene shows
the regatta at about the time of Wordsworth's death. In 1825 he had assisted
'Christopher North' to organize a regatta to welcome Scott and Canning to the
Lakes. *Opposite above*: The lakes of Ennerdale, Buttermere, Crummock and
Loweswater can all be seen, from a point high up on Brandreth, where the party
seems to be preparing for a picnic. *Opposite below*: Thirlmere and Wytheburn.
The hampers, the books and the canvas windscreen have been brought up some
way from the road for a family picnic on the fell-side.

The magnificent lithographs, reproduced from J. B. Pyne's *The English Lake District*, were not published until three years after Wordsworth's death; but they show his 'dear native regions' as they were at the end of his life—the railway train, against which he fought so vigorously, puffs serenely out of Windermere station; a family party picnic on the fells above Thirlmere (soon to become a reservoir); tourists high above Ennerdale and Buttermere relax on the remote slopes of Brandreth; visitors are lavishly entertained by the glories of the Windermere regatta. Soon they will be recalling their visits with photographic records. In Wordsworth's words the Lake District is becoming 'a sort of national property, in which every man has a right and interest who has an eye to perceive and a heart to enjoy'.

The 'Discovery' is complete; the spirit of adventure of the early travellers in pursuit of the Picturesque, the Sublime and the Beautiful has given place to the easy confidence of Victorian holiday-makers seeking recreation in surroundings sanctified by the poetry of Wordsworth.

Editorial Note

The enjoyable task of choosing the illustrations for this book has been greatly helped by three recent exhibitions in the Lake District. In 1980 'The View Finders, an Exhibition of Lake District Landscapes', at The Abbot Hall Art Gallery in Kendal, brought together nine well known views as portrayed by a hundred artists. I owe the Director of the Gallery, Mary Burkett, a debt of gratitude for assembling and cataloguing such a splendid collection of images of the Lake District, and for help over the choice of illustrations for this volume, several of which are from the permanent collection at Abbot Hall.

This book inevitably runs parallel to two exhibitions, in which I have been involved, at the Grasmere and Wordsworth Museum at Dove Cottage, in 1982 and 1983. 'The Discovery of the Lake District, 1750–1810, a Context for Wordsworth' and 'The Lake District Discovered, 1810–1850, The Artists, The Tourists and Wordsworth' related the artistic interpretation of the Lakes to the life and work of Wordsworth, as do the illustrations in this book. Access to the Museum's photographic catalogue of Lake District pictures has simplified their selection. I am particularly grateful to the staff of both the Library and the Museum at Dove Cottage for skilful and patient help, and above all to Robert Woof, the Secretary and Keeper of the Collection of the Trustees of Dove Cottage. He initiated and inspired the two exhibitions, and his perceptive and inexhaustible enthusiasm have led me to many images which otherwise I would have missed. As an amateur in the field of Wordsworth scholarship, I only hope that a little of his unique knowledge of Wordsworth and his circle, and their relationship with the Lake District, has rubbed off on me. Both he and Janet Adam Smith have with great generosity conscientiously read and commented on the draft of my introduction. Professor Alan Hill has also proffered invaluable suggestions which I have adopted with gratitude.

A page of Dorothy Wordsworth's original manuscript of her account of an excursion to the top of Scawfell Pike in 1818, versions of which were included by Wordsworth as appendices to the 1823 and 1835 editions of the *Guide*.

A

GUIDE

THROUGH THE

DISTRICT OF THE LAKES

IN

The North of England,

WITH

A DESCRIPTION OF THE SCENERY, &c.

FOR THE USE OF

TOURISTS AND RESIDENTS.

FIFTH EDITION,
WITH CONSIDERABLE ADDITIONS.

By WILLIAM WORDSWORTH.

KENDAL:
PUBLISHED BY HUDSON AND NICHOLSON,
AND IN LONDON BY
LONGMAN & CO., MOXON, AND WHITTAKER & CO.
1835.

DIRECTIONS AND INFORMATION FOR THE TOURIST

In preparing this Manual, it was the Author's principal wish to furnish a Guide or Companion for the *Minds* of Persons of taste, and feeling for Landscape, who might be inclined to explore the District of the Lakes with that degree of attention to which its beauty may fairly lay claim. For the more sure attainment, however, of this primary object, he will begin by undertaking the humble and tedious task of supplying the Tourist with directions how to approach the several scenes in their best, or most convenient, order. But first, supposing the approach to be made from the south, and through Yorkshire, there are certain interesting spots which may be confidently recommended to his notice, if time can be spared before entering upon the Lake District; and the route may be changed in returning.

There are three approaches to the Lakes through Yorkshire; the least adviseable is the great north road by Catterick and Greta Bridge, and onwards to Penrith. The Traveller, however, taking this route, might halt at Greta Bridge, and be well recompenced if he can afford to give an hour or two to the banks of the Greta, and of the Tees, at Rokeby. Barnard Castle also, about two miles up the Tees, is a striking object, and the main North Road might be rejoined at Bowes. Every one has heard of the great fall of the Tees above Middleham, interesting for its grandeur, as the avenue of rocks that leads to it, is to the geologist. But this place lies so far out of the way as scarcely to be within the compass of our notice. It might, however, be visited by a Traveller on foot, or on horseback, who could rejoin the main road upon Stanemoor.

The second road leads through a more interesting tract of country, beginning at Ripon, from which place see Fountain's Abbey, and thence by Hackfall, and Masham, to Jervaux Abbey, and up the vale of Wensley; turning aside before Askrigg is reached, to see Aysgarth-force, upon the Ure; and again, near Hawes, to Hardraw Scar, of which, with its waterfall, Turner has a fine drawing. Thence over the fells to Sedbergh, and Kendall.

The third approach from Yorkshire is through Leeds. Four miles beyond that town are the ruins of Kirkstall Abbey, should that road to Skipton be chosen; but the other by Otley may be made much more interesting by turning off at Addington to Bolton Bridge, for the sake of visiting the Abbey and grounds. It would be well, however, for a party

34

Below: Dungeon Ghyll, Langdale, by L. Aspland. 'Into a chasm a mighty block/Hath fallen, and made a bridge of rock;/The gulf is deep below:/And, in a basin black and small, Receives a lofty waterfall.' *The Idle Shepherd-Boys*.

Right: Morning amongst the Coniston Fells, by J. M. W. Turner. This painting which resulted from Turner's tour of the Lakes in 1797 was exhibited at the Royal Academy in 1798, accompanied by a passage from Milton's *Paradise Lost*, 'Ye mists and exhalations that now arise/From hill or steaming lake. . . .' Wordsworth in the drafts for *The Prelude* which he was writing in Germany, at the same time, was struggling with exactly the same passage from Milton.

Above: Lake Scene in Cumberland, Evening, 1792, oil painting by Philip James de Loutherbourg. De Loutherbourg, who was born in Alsace, was closely associated with the theatre and worked for Garrick at Drury Lane. He visited the Lakes in 1783 where he probably met Gainsborough. He was much given to presenting the Salvatorian Sublime, as in this idealized view. Although it departs from any topographic exactitude it epitomizes two characteristics of the Lakes emphasized by Wordsworth in the *Guide*—that many of the lakes 'assume the resemblance of a magnificent river' and 'masses of rock, that have been precipitated from the heights into the area of waters, lie in some places like stranded ships; or have acquired the compact structure of jutting piers'.

Saddleback and part of Skiddaw, watercolour by John Constable. Constable, in his visit to the Lakes in 1806, climbed far from the beaten tracks of the tourists, and in his sketches departed far from the conventions of picturesque composition. This drawing is inscribed on the back 'Stormy Day—Noon'.

The Langdale Pikes from Lowood, oil painting by J. C. Ibbetson. Ibbetson presents probably the most painted view in the Lakes with a conventionally arranged foreground of framing trees and picturesquely grouped cows and figures. The house in the middle distance is Brathay Hall.

Esthwaite, watercolour by James Bourne. The small lake near Hawkshead was constantly in Wordsworth's sight and mind when he was attending the Grammar School and lodging with Ann Tyson.

'The Kendal Flying Machine', pen and watercolour drawing by Thomas
Rowlandson, 1820. This was the means of transport to the Lakes when the
Guide was first published. Forty years later when Wordsworth died, the railway
had reached Windermere.

previously to secure beds, if wanted, at the inn, as there is but one, and it is
much resorted to in summer.

The Traveller on foot, or horseback, would do well to follow the banks of
the Wharf upwards, to Burnsall, and thence cross over the hills to Gordale—
a noble scene, beautifully described in Gray's Tour, and with which no one
can be disappointed. Thence to Malham, where there is a respectable
village inn, and so on, by Malham Cove, to Settle.

Travellers in carriages must go from Bolton Bridge to Skipton, where
they rejoin the main road; and should they be inclined to visit Gordale, a
tolerable road turns off beyond Skipton. Beyond Settle, under Giggleswick
Scar, the road passes an ebbing and flowing well, worthy the notice of the
Naturalist. Four miles to the right of Ingleton, is Weathercote Cave, a fine
object, but whoever diverges for this, must return to Ingleton. Near
Kirkby Lonsdale observe the view from the bridge over the Lune, and
descend to the channel of the river, and by no means omit looking at the Vale
of Lune from the Church-yard.

The journey towards the lake country through Lancashire, is, with the
exception of the Vale of the Ribble, at Preston, uninteresting; till you come
near Lancaster, and obtain a view of the fells and mountains of Lancashire
and Westmorland; with Lancaster Castle, and the Tower of the Church
seeming to make part of the Castle, in the foreground.

The approach to the Lakes, Coniston Fells, watercolour by J. M. W. Turner.
After the crossing of the sands from Lancaster, Wordsworth indicates that 'the
Lakes would be advantageously approached by Coniston.'

They who wish to see the celebrated ruins of Furness Abbey, and are not
afraid of crossing the Sands, may go from Lancaster to Ulverston; from
which place take the direct road to Dalton; but by all means return through
Urswick, for the sake of the view from the top of the hill, before descending
into the grounds of Conishead Priory. From this quarter the Lakes would
be advantageously approached by Coniston; thence to Hawkshead, and by
the Ferry over Windermere, to Bowness: a much better introduction than by
going direct from Coniston to Ambleside, which ought not to be done, as that
would greatly take off from the effect of Windermere.

Let us now go back to Lancaster. The direct road thence to Kendal is 22
miles, but by making a circuit of eight miles, the Vale of the Lune to Kirkby
Lonsdale will be included. The whole tract is pleasing; there is one view
mentioned by Gray and Mason especially so. In West's Guide it is thus
pointed out: — 'About a quarter of a mile beyond the third mile-stone, where
the road makes a turn to the right, there is a gate on the left which leads into a
field where the station meant, will be found.' Thus far for those who
approach the Lakes from the South.

Travellers from the North would do well to go from Carlisle by Wigton,
and proceed along the Lake of Bassenthwaite to Keswick; or, if convenience
should take them first to Penrith, it would still be better to cross the country
to Keswick, and begin with that vale, rather than with Ulswater. It is worth
while to mention in this place, that the banks of the river Eden, about Corby,

Bassenthwaite Lake, looking south, by Thomas Allom, 'flanked by Skiddaw and Wallow Crag'. The foot of the lake is only five miles from Wordsworth's birthplace.

are well worthy of notice, both on account of their natural beauty, and the viaducts which have recently been carried over the bed of the river, and over a neighbouring ravine.   In the Church of Wetherby, close by, is a fine piece of monumental sculpture by Nollekins.   The scenes of Nunnery, upon the Eden, or rather that part of them which is upon Croglin, a mountain stream there falling into the Eden, are, in their way, unrivalled.   But the nearest road thither, from Corby, is so bad, that no one can be advised to take it in a carriage.   Nunnery may be reached from Corby by making a circuit and crossing the Eden at Armathwaite bridge.   A portion of this road, however, is bad enough.

As much the greatest number of Lake Tourists begin by passing from Kendal to Bowness, upon Windermere, our notices shall commence with that Lake.   Bowness is situated upon its eastern side, and at equal distance from each extremity of the Lake of

WINDERMERE

The lower part of this Lake is rarely visited, but has many interesting points of view, especially at Storr's Hall and at Fell-foot, where the Coniston Mountains peer nobly over the western barrier, which elsewhere, along the whole Lake, is comparatively tame.   To one also who has ascended the hill from Graithwaite on the western side, the Promontory called Rawlinson's

Skelwith Force and the Langdale Pikes, by William Havell. 'The number of the torrents and smaller brooks is infinite with their water-falls and water breaks.' The Greenbarn Beck from Little Langdale descends over Colwith Force and joins Great Langdale Beck to form the River Brathay; then falls over Skelwith Force, to join the Rothay from Grasmere and Rydal Water, before flowing into Windermere.

Nab, Storr's Hall, and the Troutbeck Mountains, about sun-set, make a splendid landscape. The view from the Pleasure-house of the Station near the Ferry has suffered much from Larch plantations; this mischief, however, is gradually disappearing, and the Larches, under the management of the proprietor, Mr. Curwen, are giving way to the native wood. Windermere ought to be seen both from its shores and from its surface. None of the other Lakes unfold so many fresh beauties to him who sails upon them. This is owing to its greater size, to the islands, and to its having *two* vales at the head, with their accompanying mountains of nearly equal dignity. Nor can the grandeur of these two terminations be seen at once from any point, except from the bosom of the Lake. The Islands may be explored at any time of the day; but one bright unruffled evening, must if possible, be set apart for the splendour, the stillness, and solemnity of a three hour's voyage upon the higher division of the Lake, not omitting, towards the

The ferry on Windermere in 1792, by John
'Warwick' Smith. The ferry was frequently used by Wordsworth during his years at
Hawkshead—'I bounded down the hill, shouting amain/A lusty summons to the farther
shore/For the old Ferry man. . . .' It is now a car ferry and is still in regular use as a vital link
between Bowness and Hawkshead.

end of the excursion, to quit the expanse of water, and peep into the close and
calm River at the head; which, in its quiet character, at such a time, appears
rather like an overflow of the peaceful Lake itself, than to have any more
immediate connection with the rough mountains whence it has descended, or
the turbulent torrents by which it is supplied. Many persons content
themselves with what they see of Windermere during their progress in a boat
from Bowness to the head of the Lake, walking thence to Ambleside. But
the whole road from Bowness is rich in diversity of pleasing or grand scenery;
there is scarcely a field on the road side, which, if entered, would not give to
the landscape some additional charm. Low-wood Inn, a mile from the head
of Windermere, is a most pleasant halting-place; no inn in the whole district
is so agreeably situated for water views and excursions; and the fields above
it, and the lane that leads to Troutbeck, present beautiful views towards each
extremity of the Lake. From this place, and from

AMBLESIDE,

Rides may be taken in numerous directions, and the interesting walks are inexhaustible;* a few out of the main road may be particularized;—the lane that leads from Ambleside to Skelgill; the ride, or walk by Rothay Bridge, and up the stream under Loughrigg Fell, continued on the western side of Rydal Lake, and along the fell to the foot of Grasmere Lake, and thence round by the church of Grasmere; or, turning round Loughrigg Fell by Loughrigg Tarn and the River Brathay, back to Ambleside. From

Pen and ink drawing by John Harden of Wordsworth's Stamp Office,
Ambleside, in 1834. In March 1813 Wordsworth had been appointed
Distributor of Stamps for Westmorland, a post which involved much work and
some travelling; it brought in about £200 a year. The Stamp Office appears in
Harden's sketch on the right-hand side of the street which leads to Brathay and
Hawkshead.

* Mr. Green's Guide to the Lakes, in two vols., contains a complete Magazine of minute and accurate information of this kind, with the names of mountains, streams, &c.

Ambleside is another charming excursion by Clappersgate, where cross the Brathay, and proceed with the river on the right to the hamlet of Skelwith-fold; when the houses are passed, turn, before you descend the hill, through a gate on the right, and from a rocky point is a fine view of the Brathay River, Langdale Pikes, &c.; then proceed to Colwithforce, and up Little Langdale to Blea Tarn. The scene in which this small piece of water lies, suggested to the Author the following description, (given in his Poem of the Excursion) supposing the spectator to look down upon it, not from the road, but from one of its elevated sides.

Behold!
Beneath our feet, a little lowly Vale,
A lowly Vale, and yet uplifted high
Among the mountains; even as if the spot
Had been, from eldest time by wish of theirs,
So placed, to be shut out from all the world!
Urn-like it was in shape, deep as an Urn;
With rocks encompassed, save that to the South
Was one small opening, where a heath-clad ridge
Supplied a boundary less abrupt and close;
A quiet treeless nook,* with two green fields,
A liquid pool that glittered in the sun,
And one bare Dwelling; one Abode, no more!
It seemed the home of poverty and toil,
Though not of want: the little fields, made green
By husbandry of many thrifty years,
Paid cheerful tribute to the moorland House.
—There crows the Cock, single in his domain:
The small birds find in spring no thicket there
To shroud them; only from the neighbouring Vales
The Cuckoo, straggling up to the hill tops,
Shouteth faint tidings of some gladder place.

From this little Vale return towards Ambleside by Great Langdale, stopping, if there be time, to see Dungeon-ghyll waterfall.

The Lake of

CONISTON

May be conveniently visited from Ambleside, but is seen to most advantage by entering the country over the Sands from Lancaster. The Stranger, from the moment he sets his foot on those Sands, seems to leave the turmoil and traffic of the world behind him; and, crossing the majestic plain whence the sea has retired, he beholds, rising apparently from its base, the cluster of mountains among which he is going to wander, and towards whose recesses, by the Vale of Coniston, he is gradually and peacefully led. From the Inn at the head of Coniston Lake, a leisurely Traveller might have much pleasure in looking into Yewdale and Tilberthwaite, returning to his Inn from the head

---

* No longer strictly applicable, on account of recent plantations.

Above: Blea Tarn and the Langdale Pikes,
by William Green.
'So placed to be shut out from all the world.' A description of Blea Tarn from
The Excursion was included in this edition of the *Guide*.

Opposite: Birker Force in Eskdale, by Thomas Allom.
Wordsworth considered that this waterfall stood 'at the head of the finest ravine
in the country'.

of Yewdale by a mountain track which has the farm of Tarn Hows, a little on the right: by this road is seen much the best view of Coniston Lake from the south.   At the head of Coniston Water there is an agreeable Inn, from which an enterprising Tourist might go to the Vale of the Duddon, over Walna Scar, down to Seathwaite, Newfield, and to the rocks where the river issues from a narrow pass into the broad Vale.   The stream is very interesting for the space of a mile above this point, and below, by Ulpha Kirk, till it enters the Sands, where is it overlooked by the solitary Mountain Black Comb, the summit of which, as that experienced surveyor, Colonel Mudge, declared, commands a more extensive view than any point in Britain.   Ireland he saw more than once, but not when the sun was above the horizon.

> Close by the Sea, lone sentinel,
>   Black-Comb his forward station keeps;
> He breaks the sea's tumultuous swell,—
>   An ponders o'er the level deeps.
>
> He listens to the bugle horn,
>   Where Eskdale's lovely valley bends;
> Eyes Walney's early fields of corn;
>   Sea-birds to Holker's woods he sends.
>
> Beneath his feet the sunk ship rests,
> In Duddon Sands, its masts all bare:

The Minstrels of Windermere, by Chas. Farish, B.D.

The Tourist may either return to the Inn at Coniston by Broughton, or, by turning to the left before he comes to that town, or, which would be better, he may cross from

ULPHA KIRK

Over Birker moor, to Birker-force, at the head of the finest ravine in the country; and thence up the Vale of the Esk, by Hardknot and Wrynose, back to Ambleside.   Near the road, in ascending from Eskdale, are conspicuous remains of a Roman fortress.   Details of the Duddon and Donnerdale are given in the Author's series of Sonnets upon the Duddon and in the accompanying Notes.   In addition to its two Vales at its head, Windermere communicates with two lateral Vallies; that of Troutbeck, distinguished by the mountains at its head—by picturesque remains of cottage architecture; and, towards the lower part, by bold foregrounds formed by the steep and winding banks of the river.   This Vale, as before mentioned, may be most conveniently seen from Low Wood.   The other lateral Valley, that of Hawkshead, is visited to most advantage, and most conveniently, from Bowness; crossing the Lake by the Ferry—then pass the two villages of Sawrey, and on quitting the latter, you have a fine view of the Lake of Esthwaite, and the cone of one of the Langdale Pikes in the distance.
Before you leave Ambleside give three minutes to looking at a passage of the brook which runs through the town; it is to be seen from a garden on the right bank of the stream, a few steps above the bridge—the garden at present

Rydal Mount, 'Etched from Nature by William Green and Published at
Ambleside, May 1, 1821', eight years after the Wordsworths had moved in.
Green was trained as a surveyor in Liverpool. After he settled at Ambleside in
1800, he published, as well as landscapes, hundreds of prints of detailed and
accurate drawings of buildings. These have left a wonderful record of buildings
at the time Wordsworth was living at Grasmere and Rydal. Green was a
frequent visitor at Rydal Mount.

is rented by Mrs. Airey.—Stockgill-force, upon the same stream, will have
been mentioned to you as one of the sights of the neighbourhood.   And by a
Tourist halting a few days in Ambleside, the *Nook* also might be visited; a
spot where there is a bridge over Scandale-beck, which makes a pretty
subject for the pencil.   Lastly, for residents of a week or so at Ambleside,
there are delightful rambles over every part of Loughrigg Fell and among the
enclosures on its sides; particularly about Loughrigg Tarn, and on its eastern
side about Fox How and the properties adjoining to the northwards.

ROAD FROM AMBLESIDE TO KESWICK.

The Waterfalls of Rydal are pointed out to everyone.   But it ought to be
observed here, that Rydal-mere is no where seen to advantage from the *main
road*.   Fine views of it may be had from Rydal Park; but these grounds, as
well as those of Rydal Mount and Ivy Cottage, from which also it is viewed to
advantage, are private.   A foot road passing behind Rydal Mount and under
Nab Scar to Grasmere, is very favourable to views of the Lake and the Vale,
looking back towards Ambleside.   The horse road also, along the western
side of the Lake, under Loughrigg fell, as before mentioned, does justice to
the beauties of this small mere, of which the Traveller who keeps the high
road is not at all aware.

GRASMERE.

There are two small Inns in the Vale of Grasmere, one near the Church, from which it may be conveniently explored in every direction, and a mountain walk taken up Easedale Tarn, one of the finest tarns in the country, thence to Stickle Tarn, and to the top of Langdale Pikes.   See also the Vale of Grasmere from Butterlip How.   A boat is kept by the innkeeper, and this circular Vale, in the solemnity of a fine evening, will make, from the bosom of the Lake, an impression that will be scarcely ever effaced.

The direct road from Grasmere to Keswick does not (as has been observed of Rydal Mere shew to advantage Thirlmere, or Wythburn Lake, with its surrounding mountains.   By a Traveller proceeding at leisure, a deviation ought to be made from the main road, when he has advanced a little

Above: 'Thirlmere Bridge, looking North', by Thomas Allom.
The causeway which divided Thirlmere in two, before it was inundated and turned into a reservoir.

Opposite: *Ford's Guide*, 1839, one of the many pocket guides published between 1810 and 1850. William Ford, some time curate at Wythburn, Thirlmere, states his obligation to Mr Wordsworth for his 'admirably descriptive sketch,' but claims to amplify 'the slight poetical touches of the author of *The Excursion*.'

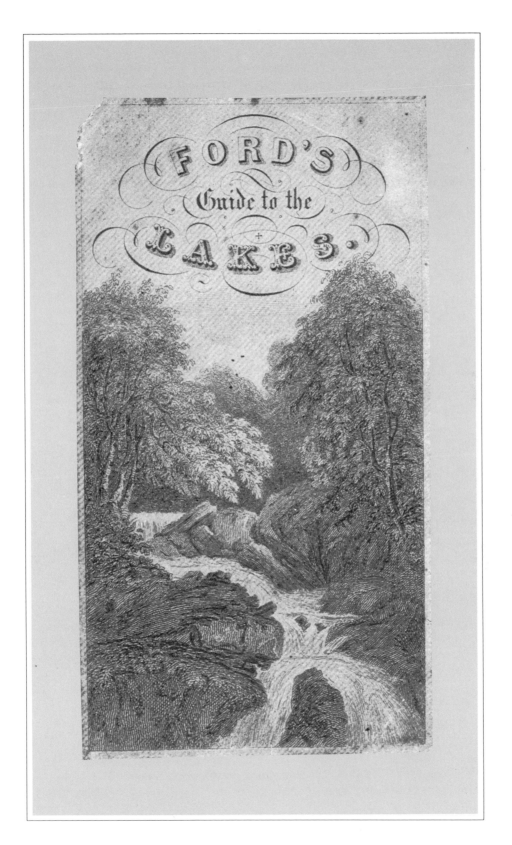

Ford's Guide to the Lakes.

beyond the sixth mile-stone short of Keswick, from which point there is a noble view of the Vale of Legberthwaite, with Blencathra (commonly called Saddle-back) in front. Having previously enquired, at the Inn near Wythburn Chapel, the best way from this mile-stone to the bridge that divides the Lake, he must cross it, and proceed with the Lake on the right, to the hamlet a little beyond Shoulthwaite Moss, about four miles from Keswick; or, if on foot, the Tourist may follow the stream that issues from Thirlmere down the romantic Vale of St. John's, and so (enquiring the way at some cottage) to Keswick, by a circuit of little more than a mile. A more interesting tract of country is scarcely any where to be seen, than the road between Ambleside and Keswick, with the deviations that have been pointed out. Helvellyn may be conveniently ascended from the Inn at Wythburn.

'Castle Rock, Vale of St John, looking South' by Thomas Allom.

'. . . midmost of the vale, a mound
Arose, with airy turrets crown'd
Buttress and rampires circling bound
And mightly keep and tower.'

Walter Scott, 'The Bridal of Triermain'. The legend is that when the earth
is approached it disappears and all that is left is the rocky eminence.
It is the scene of Scott's 'Bridal of Triermain', to which the two
Arthurian knights in Allom's picture refer.

THE VALE OF KESWICK.

This Vale stretches, without winding, nearly North and South, from the head of Derwent Water to the foot of Bassenthwaite Lake. It communicates with Borrowdale on the South; with the river Greta, and Thirlmere, on the East, with which the Traveller has become acquainted on his way from Ambleside; and with the Vale of Newlands on the West—which last Vale he may pass through, in going to, or returning from, Buttermere. The best views of Keswick Lake are from Crow Park; Frier's Crag; the Stable-field, close by; the Vicarage, and from various points in taking the circuit of the Lake. More distant views, and perhaps full as interesting, are from the side of Latrigg, from Ormathwaite, and Applethwaite; and thence along the road

The Vale of Keswick and Crosthwaite church from Applethwaite by Henry Gastineau. Wordsworth describes this hamlet of six or seven houses, 'you look out from this chink or fissure, which is sprinkled with orchards and trees, and behold the whole splendour of the upper and the middle part of the Vale of Keswick, with its Lakes and Mountains spread before your eyes.' In 1803 Sir George Beaumont gave Wordsworth a property at Applethwaite, so that he could live near Coleridge; however, Wordsworth never occupied it.

The Bowder Stone by William Green, the enormous erratic block which lies in the Jaws of Borrowdale. The cottage was built by Joseph Pocklington to house an old woman who acted as a guide. He also cut a hole under the rock so that, as Southey put it, 'the curious may gratify themselves by shaking hands with the old woman.'

at the foot of Skiddaw towards Bassenthwaite, for about a quarter of a mile. There are fine bird's eye views from the Castle-hill; from Ashness, on the road to Watenlath, and by following the Watenlath stream downwards to the Cataract of Lodore. This Lake also, if the weather be fine, ought to be circumnavigated. There are good views along the western side of Bassenthwaite Lake, and from Armathwaite at its foot; but the eastern side from the high road has little to recommend it. The Traveller from Carlisle, approaching by way of Ireby has, from the old road on the top of Bassenthwaite-hawse, much the most striking view of the Plain and Lake of Bassenthwaite, flanked by Skiddaw, and terminated by Wallowcrag on the south-east of Derwent Lake; the same point commands an extensive view of Solway Frith and the Scotch Mountains. They who take the circuit of Derwent Lake, may at the same time include BORROWDALE, going as far as Bowder-stone, or Rosthwaite. Borrowdale is also conveniently seen on the way to Wastdale over Styhead; or, to Buttermere, by Seatoller and Honister Crag; or, going over the Stake, through Langdale, to Amble-

Two views of Ambleside in 1786, watercolours by Francis Towne. 'The objection to white, as a colour in large spots or masses in landscape, especially in mountainous country are insurmountable . . . . Five or six white houses, scattered over a valley, by their obtrusiveness, dot the surface, and divide it into triangles, or other mathematical figures, haunting the eye and disturbing the repose which might otherwise be perfect.' Towne's drawings demonstrate how acceptable the white houses can be in the Lake District landscape.

Scawdale Beck by William Green. This turbulent stream joins the Rothay near Miller Bridge, only about a mile from Rydal Mount.

A view of Derwentwater in 1809, watercolour signed J.G. (probably Joshua Green). Looking to the head of the lake from the western shore. The building in the distance is Barrow Cascade House, to which the eccentric Joseph Pocklington retired after he sold his island house to Lieut.-Colonel (later General) William Peachy in 1796.

Keswick as it was at the time of Wordsworth's death, by Theophilus Lindsay Aspland. The church of St John the Evangelist was built in 1838. Bassenthwaite can be seen in the distance.

Honister Crag by Thomas Allom. 'The descent into Gatesgarth, immediately under Honister Crag, causes one of the sublimest impressions which this country can produce.' The sublimity of the scene has been emphasized by the introduction of a foray at the summit of the pass. The crag has been developed as a quarry for the beautiful Honister green slates since the seventeenth century.

side. Buttermere may be visited by a shorter way through Newlands, but though the descent upon the Vale of Buttermere, by this approach, is very striking, as it also is to one entering by the head of the Vale, under Honister Crag, yet, after all, the best entrance from Keswick is from the lower part of the Vale, having gone over Whinlater to Scale Hill, where there is a roomy Inn, with very good accommodation. The Mountains of the Vale of

BUTTERMERE AND CRUMMOCK

Are no where so impressive as from the bosom of Crummock Water. Scale-force, near it, is a fine chasm, with a lofty, though but slender, fall of water.

From Scale Hill a pleasant walk may be taken to an eminence in Mr.

Gatesgarth-dale as William Gilpin saw it. He found it 'a very tremendous
scene'. This is the valley that descends to Buttermere from Honister Pass.
Gilpin has shown his complete disregard for topographical accuracy in the way
he has distorted nature. The impending rocks are shown as Gray had seen
them—'hanging loose and nodding forwards'.

Marshall's woods, and another by crossing the bridge at the foot of the hill,
upon which the Inn stands, and turning to the right, after the opposite hill
has been ascended a little way, then follow the road for half a mile or so that
leads towards Lorton, looking back upon Crummock Water, &c., between
the openings of the fences.   Turn back and make your way to

LOWESWATER.

But this small Lake is only approached to advantage from the other end;
therefore any Traveller going by this road to Wastdale, must look back upon
it.   This road to Wastdale, after passing the village of Lamplugh Cross,
presents suddenly a fine view of the lake of Ennerdale, with its Mountains;
and, six or seven miles beyond, leads down upon Calder Abbey.   Little of
this ruin is left, but that little is well worthy of notice.   At Calder Bridge are
two comfortable Inns, and, a few miles beyond, accommodations may be had
at the Strands, at the foot of Wastdale.   Into

WASTDALE

Are three horse-roads, viz. over the Stye from Borrowdale; a short cut from
Eskdale by Burnmoor Tarn, which road descends upon the head of the Lake;
and the principal entrance from the open country by the Strands at its
foot.   This last is much the best approach.   Wastdale is well worth the

notice of the Traveller who is not afraid of fatigue; no part of the country is more distinguished by sublimity. Wastwater may also be visited from Ambleside; by going up Langdale, over Hardknot and Wrynose—down Eskdale and by Irton Hall to the Strands; but this road can only be taken on foot, or on horseback or in a cart.

We will conclude with

ULLSWATER,

As being, perhaps, upon the whole, the happiest combination of beauty and grandeur, which any of the Lakes affords. It lies not more than ten miles from Ambleside, and the Pass of Kirkstone and the descent from it are very impressive; but, notwithstanding, this Vale, like the others, loses much of its effect by being entered from the head: so that it is better to go from Keswick through Matterdale, and descend upon Gowbarrow Park; you are thus brought at once upon a magnificent view of the two higher reaches of the

Wastdale Head, pen and wash drawing by
Joseph Farington. 'No part of the country is more distinguished by sublimity.'
The prominent mountain is Great Gable, the hub of the Lake District.

Lake.   Ara-force thunders down the Ghyll on the left, at a small distance from the road.   If Ullswater be approached from Penrith, a mile and a half brings you to the winding vale of Eamont, and the prospects increase in interest till you reach Patterdale; but the first four miles along Ullswater by this road are comparatively tame; and in order to see the lower part of the Lake to advantage, it is necessary to go round by Pooley Bridge, and to ride at least three miles along the Westmorland side of the water, towards Martindale.   The views, especially if you ascend from the road into the fields, are magnificent; yet this is only mentioned that the transient Visitant may know what exists; for it would be inconvenient to go in search of them.   They who take this course of three or four miles *on foot*, should have a boat in readiness at the end of the walk, to carry them across to the Cumberland side of the Lake, near Old Church, thence to pursue the road upwards to Patterdale.   The Church-yard Yew-tree still survives at Old Church, but there are no remains of a Place of Worship, a New Chapel having been erected in a more central situation, which Chapel was consecrated by the then Bishop of Carlisle, when on his way to crown Queen Elizabeth, he being the only Prelate who would undertake the office.   It may be here mentioned that Bassenthwaite Chapel yet stands in a bay as sequestered as the Site of Old Church; such situations having been chosen in disturbed times to elude marauders.

The Trunk, or Body of the Vale of Ullswater need not be further noticed, as its beauties show themselves: but the curious Traveller may wish to know something of its tributary Streams.

At Dalemain, about three miles from Penrith, a Stream is crossed called the Dacre, or Dacor, which name it bore as early as the time of the Venerable Bede.   This stream does not enter the Lake, but joins the Eamont a mile below.   It rises in the moorish Country about Penruddock, flows down a soft sequestered Valley, passing by the ancient mansions of Hutton John and Dacre Castle.   The former is pleasantly situated, though of a character somewhat gloomy and monastic, and from some of the fields near Dalemain, Dacre Castle, backed by the jagged summit of Saddleback, with the Valley and Stream in front, forms a grand picture.   There is no other stream that conducts to any glen or valley worthy of being mentioned, till we reach that which leads up to Ara-force, and thence into Matterdale, before spoken of.   Matterdale, though a wild and interesting spot, has no peculiar features that would make it worth the Stranger's while to go in search of them; but, in Gowbarrow Park, the lover of Nature might linger for hours.   Here is a powerful Brook, which dashes among rocks through a deep glen, hung on every side with a rich and happy intermixture of native wood; here are beds of luxuriant fern, aged hawthorns, and hollies decked with honeysuckles; and fallow-deer glancing and bounding over the lawns and through the

Opposite: Aira Force, by Thomas Allom, the scene of Wordsworth's poem
'The Somnambulist'.
'List ye who pass by Lyulph's Tower/At eve; how softly then/Doth Aira-force,
that torrent hoarse,/Speak from the woody glen!'

thickets. These are the attractions of the retired views, or constitute a foreground for ever-varying pictures of the majestic Lake, forced to take a winding course by bold promontories, and environed by mountains of sublime form, towering above each other. At the outlet of Gowbarrow Park, we reach a third stream, which flows through a little recess called Glencoin, where lurks a single house, yet visible from the road. Let the Artist or leisurely Traveller turn aside to it, for the buildings and objects around them are romantic and picturesque. Having passed under the steeps of Styebarrow Crag, and the remains of its native woods, at Glenridding Bridge, a fourth Stream is crossed.

The opening on the side of Ullswater Vale, down which this Stream flows, is adorned with fertile fields, cottages, and natural groves, that agreeably unite with the transverse views of the Lake; and the Stream, if followed up after the enclosures are left behind, will lead along bold water-breaks and waterfalls to a silent Tarn in the recesses of Helvellyn. This desolate spot was formerly haunted by eagles, that built in the precipice which forms its western barrier. These birds used to wheel and hover round the head of the solitary angler. It also derives a melancholy interest from the fate of a young man, a stranger, who perished some years ago, by falling down the rocks in his attempt to cross over to Grasmere. His remains were discovered by means of a faithful dog that had lingered here for the space of three months, self-supported, and probably retaining to the last an attachment to the skeleton of its master. But to return to the road in the main Vale of Ullswater.—At the head of the Lake (being now in Patterdale) we cross a fifth Stream, Grisdale Beck: this would conduct through a woody steep, where may be seen some unusually large ancient hollies, up to the level area of the Valley of Grisdale; hence there is a path for foot-travellers, and along which a horse may be led, to Grasmere. A sublime combination of mountain forms appears in front while ascending the bed of this valley, and the impression increases till the path leads almost immediately under the projecting masses of Helvellyn. Having retraced the banks of the Stream to Patterdale, and pursued the road up the main Dale, the next considerable stream would, if ascended in the same manner, conduct to Deep-dale, the character of which Valley may be conjectured from its name. It is terminated by a cove, a craggy and gloomy abyss, with precipitous sides; a faithful receptacle of the snows that are driven into it, by the west wind, from the summit of Fairfield. Lastly, having gone along the western side of Brotherswater and passed Hartsop Hall, a Stream soon after issues from a cove richly decorated with native wood. This spot is, I believe, never explored by Travellers; but, from these sylvan and rocky recesses, whoever looks back on the gleaming surface of Brotherswater, or forward to the

Opposite: 'The unfortunate tourist of Helvellyn & his faithful dog.' In April 1805 Charles Gough, a young visitor from Manchester, lost his way in a snow storm on Striding Edge and fell from Red Cove Crag 600 feet towards Red Tarn. His body, wasted to a skeleton, was found three months later, still guarded by his faithful Irish terrier, Foxey.

Red Tarn, by T. H. Fielding, 'a silent Tarn in the recesses of Helvellyn.' This is
the scene of the melancholy story of Charles Gough and his faithful dog,
commemorated in Wordsworth's poem 'Fidelity' and Walter Scott's 'Helvellyn'.
A passage from 'Fidelity' is included in the *Guide*. Scott had visited Grasmere in
October 1805 (the year of the fatality) and together with Wordsworth and
Humphry Davy had ascended Helvellyn. Striding Edge from which Gough fell
is to the left of the tarn, Helvellyn beyond.

precipitous sides and lofty ridges of Dove Crag, &c., will be equally pleased with the beauty, the grandeur, and the wildness of the scenery.

Seven Glens or Vallies have been noticed, which branch off from the Cumberland side of the Vale. The opposite side has only two Streams of any importance, one of which would lead up from the point where it crosses the Kirkstone-road, near the foot of Brotherswater, to the decaying hamlet of Hartsop, remarkable for its cottage architecture, and thence to Hayswater, much frequented by anglers. The other, coming down Martindale, enters Ullswater at Sandwyke, opposite to Gowbarrow Park. No persons but such as come to Patterdale, merely to pass through it, should fail to walk as far as Blowick, the only enclosed land which on this side borders the higher part of the Lake. The axe has here indiscriminately levelled a rich wood of birches and oaks, that divided this favoured spot into a hundred pictures. It has yet its land-locked bays, and rock promontories; but those beautiful woods are gone, which *perfected* its seclusion; and scenes, that might formerly have been compared to an inexhaustible volume, are now spread before the eye in a single sheet,—magnificent indeed, but seemingly perused in a moment! From Blowick a narrow track conducts along the craggy side of Place-fell, richly adorned with juniper, and sprinkled over with birches, to the village of Sandwyke, a few straggling houses, that with the small estates attached to them, occupy an opening opposite to Lyulph's Tower and Gowbarrow Park. In Martindale,* the road loses sight of the lake, and leads over a steep hill, bringing you again into view of Ullswater. Its lowest reach, four miles in length, is before you; and the view terminated by the long ridge of Cross Fell in the distance. Immediately under the eye is a deep-indented bay, with a plot of fertile land, traversed by a small brook, and rendered cheerful by two or three substantial houses of a more ornamented and showy appearance than is usual in those wild spots.

From Pooley Bridge, at the foot of the Lake, Haweswater may be conveniently visited. Haweswater is a lesser Ullswater, with this advantage, that it remains undefiled by the intrusion of bad taste.

Lowther Castle is about four miles from Pooley Bridge, and, if during this Tour the Stranger has complained, as he will have had reason to do, of a want of majestic trees, he may be abundantly recompensed for his loss in the far-spreading woods which surround that mansion. Visitants, for the most part, see little of the beauty of these magnificent grounds, being content with the view from the Terrace; but the whole course of the Lowther, from Askham to the bridge under Brougham Hall, presents almost at every step some new feature of river, woodland, and rocky landscape. A portion of this tract has, from its beauty, acquired the name of the Elysian Fields;—but the course of the stream can only be followed by the pedestrian.

Note. *Vide* p.47.—About 200 yards beyond the last house on the Keswick side of Rydal village the road is cut through a low wooded rock, called Thrang Crag. The top of it, which is only a few steps on the south side, affords the best view of the Vale which is to be had by a Traveller who confines himself to the public road.

* See Page 169.

DESCRIPTION
OF THE
SCENERY OF THE LAKES
SECTION FIRST

VIEW OF THE COUNTRY AS FORMED BY NATURE

At Lucerne, in Switzerland, is shewn a Model of the Alpine country which encompasses the lake of the four Cantons. The Spectator ascends a little platform, and sees mountains, lakes, glaciers, rivers, woods, waterfalls, and vallies, with their cottages, and every other object contained in them, lying at his feet; all things being represented in their appropriate colours. It may be easily conceived that this exhibition affords an exquisite delight to the imagination, tempting it to wander at will from valley to valley, from mountain to mountain, through the deepest recesses of the Alps. But it supplies also a more substantial pleasure: for the sublime and beautiful region, with all its hidden treasures, and their bearings and relations to each other, is thereby comprehended and understood at once.

Something of this kind, without touching upon minute details and individualities which would only confuse and embarrass, will here be attempted, in respect of the Lakes in the north of England, and the vales and mountains enclosing and surrounding them. The delineation, if tolerably executed, will, in some instances, communicate to the traveller, who has already seen the objects, new information; and will assist in giving to his recollections a more orderly arrangement than his own opportunities of observing may have permitted him to make; while it will be still more useful to the future traveller, by directing his attention at once to distinctions in things which, without such previous aid, a length of time only could enable him to discover. It is hoped, also, that this Essay may become generally serviceable, by leading to habits of more exact and considerate observation than, as far as the writer knows, have hitherto been applied to local scenery.

To begin, then, with the main outlines of the country;—I know not how to give the reader a distinct image of these more readily, than by requesting him to place himself with me, in imagination, upon some given point; let it be the top of either of the mountains, Great Gavel, or Scawfell; or, rather, let us suppose our station to be a cloud hanging midway between those two mountains, at not more than half a mile's distance from the summit of each, and not many yards above their highest elevation; we shall then see stretched at our feet a number of vallies, not fewer than eight, diverging from the point, on which we are supposed to stand, like spokes from the nave of a wheel.   First, we note, lying to the south-east, the vale of Langdale*, which will conduct the eye to the long lake of Winandermere, stretched nearly to the sea; or rather to the sands of the vast bay of Morcamb, serving here for the rim of this imaginary wheel;—let us trace it in a direction from the south-east towards the south, and we shall next fix our eyes upon the vale of Coniston, running up likewise from the sea, but not (as all the other vallies do) to the nave of the wheel, and therefore it may be not inaptly represented as a broken spoke sticking in the rim.   Looking forth again, with an inclination towards the west, we see immediately at our feet the vale of Duddon, in which is no lake, but a copious stream winding among fields, rocks, and mountains, and terminating its course in the sands of Duddon.   The fourth vale, next to be observed, viz. that of the Esk, is of the same general character as the last yet beautifully discriminated from it by peculiar features.   Its stream passes under the woody steep upon which stands Muncaster Castle, the ancient seat of the Penningtons, and after forming a short and narrow æstuary enters the sea below the small town of Ravenglass.   Next, almost due west, look down into, and along the deep valley of Wastdale, with its little chapel and half a dozen neat dwellings scattered upon a plain of meadow and corn-ground intersected with stone walls apparently innumerable, like a large piece of lawless patch-work, or an array of mathematical figures, such as in the ancient schools of geometry might have been sportively and fantastically traced out upon sand.   Beyond this little fertile plain lies, within a bed of steep mountains, the long, narrow, stern, and desolate lake of Wastdale; and, beyond this, a dusky tract of level ground conducts the eye to the Irish Sea.   The stream that issues from Wast-water is named the Irt, and falls into the æstuary of the river Esk.   Next comes in view Ennerdale, with its lake of bold and somewhat savage shores.   Its stream, the Ehen or Enna, flowing through a soft and fertile country, passes the town of Egremont, and the ruins of the castle,—then, seeming, like the other rivers, to break through the barrier of sand thrown up by the winds on this tempestuous coast, enters the Irish Sea.   The vale of Buttermere, with the lake and village of that name, and Crummock-water, beyond, next present themselves.   We will follow the main stream, the Coker, through the fertile and beautiful vale of Lorton, till it is lost in the Derwent, below the noble ruins of Cockermouth Castle.   Lastly, Borrowdale, of which the vale of Keswick is only a continuation, stretching due north, brings us to a point nearly opposite to the vale of Winandermere with which we began.   From this it will appear that the image of a wheel, thus far exact, is little more than one half complete; but the deficiency on the eastern side may be supplied by the vales of Wytheburn, Ulswater, Hawswater, and the vale of Grasmere and Rydal; none of these, however, run up to the central point between Great Gavel and Scawfell.   From this, hitherto our central point, take a flight of not more than four or five miles eastward to the ridge of Helvellyn, and you will look down upon Wytheburn and St. John's Vale, which are a branch of the vale of

---

* Anciently spelt Langden, and so called by the old inhabitants to this day—*dean*, from which the latter part of the word is derived, being in many parts of England a name for a valley.

Two views of Ennerdale, the scene of Wordsworth's poem 'The Brothers',
based on the story of a shepherd who lost his life on 'one particular rock/That
rises like a column from the vale,/Whence by our shepherds it is called THE
PILLAR.' *Above*: Print by Thomas Smith, 1767. *Opposite*: Pencil drawing by
Edward Lear, 1836. Smith romanticizes 'the lake of bold and somewhat savage
shores', with a Salvatorian dead tree and a dramatically exaggerated Pillar Rock.
Lear also shows the Pillar, but sensitively traces the curve of the ice-worn valley
(now insensitively destroyed by afforestation), so characteristic of the Lakes,
and of Lear's draughtsmanship.

Keswick; upon Ulswater, stretching due east:— and not far beyond to the south-east (though from this point not visible) lie the vale and lake of Hawswater; and lastly, the vale of Grasmere, Rydal, and Ambleside, brings you back to Winandermere, thus completing, though on the eastern side in somewhat irregular manner, the representative figure of the wheel.

Such, concisely given, is the general topographical view of the country of

the Lakes in the north of England; and it may be observed, that, from the circumference to the centre, that is, from the sea or plain country to the mountain stations specified, there is—in the several ridges that enclose these vales, and divide them from each other, I mean in the forms and surfaces, first of the swelling grounds, next of the hills and rocks, and lastly of the mountains—an ascent of almost regular gradation, from elegance and richness, to their highest point of grandeur and sublimity. It follows therefore from this, first, that these rocks, hills, and mountains, must present themselves to view in stages rising above each other, the mountains clustering together towards the central point; and next, that an observer familiar with the several vales, must, from their various position in relation to the sun, have had before his eyes every possible embellishment of beauty, dignity, and splendour, which light and shadow can bestow upon objects, so diversified. For example, in the vale of Winandermere, if the spectator looks for gentle and lovely scenes, his eye is turned towards the south; if for the grand, towards the north: in the vale of Keswick, which (as hath been said) lies almost due north of this, it is directly the reverse. Hence, when the sun is setting in summer far to the north-west, it is seen, by the spectator

Buttermere in the early 1840s, by J. B. Pyne. Compare Pyne's theatrical storm
with the luminous shower of Turner's picture of Buttermere.

from the shores or breast of Winandermere, resting among the summits of the loftiest mountains, some of which will perhaps be half or wholly hidden by clouds, or by the blaze of light which the orb diffuses around it; and the surface of the lake will reflect before the eye correspondent colours through every variety of beauty, and through all degrees of splendour.   In the vale of Keswick, at the same period, the sun sets over the humbler regions of the landscape, and showers down upon *them* the radiance which at once veils and glorifies,—sending forth, meanwhile, broad streams of rosy, crimson, purple, or golden light, towards the grand mountains in the south and south-east, which, thus illuminated, with all their projections and cavities, and with an intermixture of solemn shadows, are seen distinctly through a cool and clear atmosphere.   Of course, there is as marked a difference between the *noontide* appearance of these two opposite vales.   The bedimming haze that overspreads the south, and the clear atmosphere and determined shadows of the clouds in the north, at the same time of the day, are each seen in these several vales, with a contrast as striking.   The reader will easily conceive in what degree the intermediate vales partake of a kindred variety.

I do not indeed know of any tract of country in which, within so narrow a compass, may be found an equal variety in the influences of light and shadow upon the sublime or beautiful features of landscape; and it is owing to the combined circumstances to which the reader's attention has been directed.   From a point between Great Gavel and Scawfell, a shepherd would not require more than an hour to descend into any one of eight of the principal vales by which he would be surrounded; and all the others lie (with the exeption of Hawswater) at but a small distance.   Yet, though clustered together, every valley has its distinct and separate character: in some instances, as if they had been formed in studied contrast to each other, and in others with the united pleasing differences and resemblances of a sisterly rivalship.   This concentration of interest gives to the country a decided superiority over the most attractive districts of Scotland and Wales, especially for the pedestrian traveller.   In Scotland and Wales are found, undoubtedly, individual scenes, which, in their several kinds, cannot be excelled.   But, in Scotland, particularly, what long tracts of desolate country intervene! so that the traveller, when he reaches a spot deservedly of great celebrity, would find it difficult to determine how much of his pleasure is owing to excellence inherent in the landscape itself; and how much to an instantaneous recovery from an oppression left upon his spirits by the barrenness and desolation through which he has passed.

But to proceed with our survey;—and, first, of the MOUNTAINS.   Their *forms* are endlessly diversified, sweeping easily or boldly in simple majesty, abrupt and precipitous, or soft and elegant.   In magnitude and grandeur they are individually inferior to the most celebrated of those in some other parts of this island; but, in the combinations which they make, towering above each other, or lifting themselves in ridges like the waves of a tumultuous sea, and in the beauty and variety of their surfaces and colours, they are surpassed by none.

The general *surface* of the mountains is turf, rendered rich and green by the moisture of the climate.   Sometimes the turf, as in the neighbourhood of

Newlands, is little broken, the whole covering being soft and downy pasturage. In other places rocks predominate; the soil is laid bare by torrents and burstings of water from the sides of the mountains in heavy rains; and not unfrequently their perpendicular sides are seamed by ravines (formed also by rains and torrents) which, meeting in angular points, entrench and scar the surface with numerous figures like the letters W. and Y.

In the ridge that divides Eskdale from Wasdale, granite is found; but the Mountains are for the most part composed of the stone by mineralogists termed schist, which, as you approach the plain country, gives place to limestone and free-stone; but schist being the substance of the mountains, the predominant *colour* of their *rocky* parts is bluish, or hoary grey—the general tint of the lichens with which the bare stone is encrusted. With this blue or grey colour is frequently intermixed a red tinge, proceeding from the iron that interveins the stone, and impregnates the soil. The iron is the principle of decomposition in these rocks; and hence, when they become pulverized, the elementary particles crumbling down, overspread in many places the steep and almost precipitous sides of the mountains with an intermixture of colours, like the compound hues of a dove's neck. When in the heat of advancing summer, the fresh green tint of the herbage has somewhat faded, it is again revived by the appearance of the fern profusely spread over the same ground: and, upon this plant, more than upon any thing else, do the changes which the seasons make in the colouring of the mountains depend. About the first week in October, the rich green, which prevailed through the whole summer, is usually passed away. The brilliant and various colours of the fern are then in harmony with the autumnal woods; bright yellow or lemon colour, at the base of the mountains, melting gradually, through orange, to a dark russet brown towards the summits, where the plant, being more exposed to the weather, is in a more advanced state of decay. Neither heath nor furze are *generally* found upon the *sides* of these mountains, though in many places they are adorned by those plants, so beautiful when in flower. We may add, that the mountains are of height sufficient to have the surface towards the summit softened by distance, and to imbibe the finest aërial hues. In common also with other mountains, their apparent forms and colours are perpetually changed by the clouds and vapours which float round them: the effect indeed of mist or haze, in a country of this character, is like that of magic. I have seen six or seven ridges rising above each other, all created in a moment by the vapours upon the side of a mountain, which, in its ordinary appearance, shewed not a projecting point to furnish even a hint for such an operation.

I will take this opportunity of observing, that they who have studied the appearances of nature feel that the superiority, in point of visual interest, of mountainous over other countries—is more strikingly displayed in winter than in summer. This, as must be obvious, is partly owing to the *forms* of the mountains, which, of course, are not affected by the seasons; but also, in no small degree, to the greater variety that exists in their winter than their summer *colouring*. This variety is such, and so harmoniously preserved, that it leaves little cause of regret when the splendour of autumn is passed away. The oak-coppices, upon the sides of the mountains, retain russet

Keswick, watercolour by Edward Lear, looking across the foot of Derwentwater, Causey Pike and Grasmoor. Dated 24 September 1836. The heavy use of watercolour, unusual for Lear, evokes a typical lakeland day, with rain-laden clouds.

View from Skiddaw over Derwentwater, watercolour by Thomas Hearne, *c.* 1777. 'The form of the lake is most perfect when, ... it least resembles that of a river;—I mean, when being looked at from any given point where the whole may be seen at once.'

Derwentwater and Skiddaw, watercolour by Joseph Farington, *c.* 1760. Farington was the first well-known artist to work in the Lakes. He resided there in 1776–80, and paid many other visits. This picture of Gray's 'Elysium' conforms with the conventional picturesque formula of framing trees and figures in the foreground, a middle distance, and mountains closing the distant view.

Doctor Syntax sketching the Lake, by Rowlandson. Combe and Rowlandson's *The Tour of Doctor Syntax, in Search of the Picturesque* was a satire of the tours of the Rev. William Gilpin in search of 'Picturesque Beauty'. The climax of his tour was when he reached the Lake of Keswick.

Patterdale Palace, watercolour by Joseph Wilkinson. This was the residence of John Mounsey, 'King of Patterdale', an eccentric Quaker dalesman who fascinated visitors to Ullswater in the later eighteenth century.

leaves; the birch stands conspicuous with its silver stem and puce-coloured twigs; the hollies, with green leaves and scarlet berries, have come forth to view from among the deciduous trees, whose summer foliage had concealed them; the ivy is now plentifully apparent upon the stems and boughs of the trees, and upon the steep rocks.   In places of the deep summer-green of the herbage and fern, many rich colours play into each other over the surface of the mountains; turf (the tints of which are interchangeably tawny-green, olive, and brown,) beds of withered fern, and grey rocks, being harmoniously blended together.   The mosses and lichens are never so fresh and flourishing as in winter, if it be not a season of frost; and their minute beauties prodigally adorn the foreground.   Wherever we turn, we find these productions of nature, to which winter is rather favourable than unkindly, scattered over the walls, banks of earth, rocks and stones, and upon the trunks of trees, with the intermixture of several species of small fern, now green and fresh; and, to the observing passenger, their forms and colours are a source of inexhaustable admiration.   Add to this the hoar-frost and snow, with all the varieties they create, and which volumes would not be sufficient to describe.   I will content myself with one instance of the colouring produced by snow, which may not be uninteresting to painters.   It is extracted from the memorandum-book of a friend; and for its accuracy I can speak, having been an eye-witness of the appearance.   "I observed," says he, "the beautiful effect of the drifted snow upon the mountains, and the perfect *tone* of colour.   From the top of the mountains downwards a rich olive was produced by the powdery snow and the grass, which olive was warmed with a little brown, and in this way harmoniously combined, by insensible gradations, with the white.   The drifting took away the monotony of snow; and the whole vale of Grasmere, seen from the terrace walk in Easedale, was as varied, perhaps more so, than even in the pomp of autumn.   In the distance was Loughrigg-Fell, the basin-wall of the lake: this, from the summit downward, was a rich orange-olive; then the lake of a bright olive-green, nearly the same tint as the snow-powdered mountain tops and high slopes in Easedale; and lastly the church, with its firs, forming the centre of the view.   Next to the church came nine distinguishable hills, six of them with woody sides turned towards us, all of them oak-copses with their bright red leaves and snow-powdered twigs; these hills—so variously situated in relation to each other, and to the view in general, so variously powdered, some only enough to give the herbage a rich brown tint, one intensely white and lighting up all the others—were yet so placed, as in the most inobtrusive manner to harmonise by contrast with a perfect naked, snowless bleak summit in the far distance."

Having spoken of the forms, surface, and colour of the mountains, let us descend into the VALES.   Though these have been represented under the general image of the spokes of a wheel, they are, for the most part, winding; the windings of many being abrupt and intricate.   And, it may be observed, that, in one circumstance, the general shape of them all has been determined by that primitive conformation through which so many became receptacles of lakes.   For they are not formed, as are most of the celebrated Welsh vallies, by an approximation of the sloping bases of the opposite mountains

Yew Tree at Blelham Tarn, by T. H. Fielding.
'This lonely Yew-tree stands/Far from all human dwelling', reminiscent of the
ancient tree which inspired Wordsworth's 'Lines Left upon a Seat in a Yew-
tree, which stands near the lake of Esthwaite, on a desolate part of the shore,
commanding a beautiful prospect.'

towards each other, leaving little more between than a channel for the passage of a hasty river; but the bottom of these vallies is mostly a spacious and gently declining area, apparently level as the floor of a temple, or the surface of a lake, and broken in many cases, by rocks and hills, which rise up like islands from the plain.   In such of the vallies as make many windings, these level areas open upon the traveller in succession, divided from each other sometimes by a mutual approximation of the hills, leaving only passage for a river, sometimes by correspondent windings, without such approximation; and sometimes by a bold advance of one mountain towards that which is opposite it.   It may here be observed with propriety that the several rocks and hills, which have been described as rising up like islands from the level area of the vale, have regulated the choice of the inhabitants in the situation of their dwellings.   Where none of these are found, and the inclination of the ground is not sufficiently rapid easily to carry off the waters, (as in the higher part of Langdale, for instance,) the houses are not sprinkled over the middle of the vales, but confined to their sides, being placed merely so far up the mountain as to be protected from the floods.   But where these rocks and hills have been scattered over the plain of the vale, (as in Grasmere, Donnerdale, Eskdale, &c.) the beauty which they give to the scene is much heightened by a single cottage, or cluster of cottages, that will be almost always found under them, or upon their sides; dryness and shelter having tempted the Dalesmen to fix their habitations there.

I shall now speak of the LAKES of this country.   The form of the lake is most perfect when, like Derwent-water, and some of the smaller lakes, it least resembles that of a river;—I mean, when being looked at from any given point where the whole may be seen at once, the width of it bears such proportion to the length, that, however the outline may be diversified by far-receding bays, it never assumes the shape of a river, and is contemplated with that placid and quiet feeling which belongs peculiarly to the lake—as a body of still water under the influence of no current; reflecting therefore the clouds, the light, and all the imagery of the sky and surrounding hills; expressing also and making visible the changes of the atmosphere, and motions of the lightest breeze, and subject to agitation only from the winds—

> The visible scene
> Would enter unawares into his mind
> With all its solemn imagery, its rocks,
> Its woods, and that uncertain heaven received
> Into the bosom of the *steady* lake!

It must be noticed, as a favourable characteristic of the lakes of this country, that, though several of the largest, such as Winandermere, Ulswater, Hawswater, do, when the whole length of them is commanded from an elevated point, loose somewhat of the peculiar form of the lake, and assume the resemblance of a magnificent river; yet, as their shape is winding, (particularly that of Ulswater and Hawswater) when the view of the whole is obstructed by those barriers which determine the windings, and the spectator is confined to one reach, the appropriate feeling is revived; and one lake may thus in succession present to the eye the essential characteristic of many.   But, though the forms of the large lakes have this advantage, it is nevertheless favourable to the beauty of the country that the largest of them are comparatively small; and that the same vale generally furnishes a succession of lakes, instead of being filled with one.   The vales in North Wales, as hath been observed, are not formed for the reception of lakes; those of Switzerland, Scotland, and this part of the North of England, *are* so formed; but, in Switzerland and Scotland, the proportion of diffused water is often too great, as at the lake of Geneva for instance, and in most of the Scotch lakes.   No doubt it sounds magnificent and flatters the imagination, to hear at a distance of expanses of water so many leagues in length and miles in width; and such ample room may be delightful to the fresh-water sailor, scudding with a lively breeze amid the rapidly-shifting scenery.   But, who ever travelled along the banks of Loch-Lomond, variegated as the lower part is by islands, without feeling that a speedier termination of the long vista of blank water would be acceptable; and without wishing for an interposition of green meadows, trees, and cottages, and a sparkling stream to run by his side?   In fact, a notion, of grandeur, as connected with magnitude, has seduced persons of taste into a general mistake upon this subject.   It is much more desirable, for the purposes of pleasure, that lakes should be numerous, and small or middle-sized, than large, not only for communication by walks and rides, but for variety, and for recurrence of similar appearances.   To illustrate this by one instance:—how pleasing is it to have a ready and frequent opportunity of watching, at the outlet of a lake, the stream pushing its way among the rocks in lively contrast with the stillness from which it has escaped; and how amusing to compare its noisy and turbulent motions with the gentle playfulness of the breezes, that may be starting up or wandering here and there over the faintly-rippled surface of the broad water!   I may add, as a general remark, that, in lakes of great width, the shores cannot be distinctly seen at the same time, and therefore contribute little to mutual illustration and ornament; and, if the opposite shores are out of sight of each other, like those of the American and Asiatic lakes, then unfortunately the traveller is reminded of a nobler object; he has the blankness of a sea-prospect without the grandeur and accompanying sense of power.

As the comparatively small size of the lakes in the North of England is favourable to the production of variegated landscape their *boundary-line* also is for the most part gracefully or boldly indented.   That uniformity which prevails in the primitive frame of the lower grounds among all chains or clusters of mountains where large bodies of still water are bedded, is broken by the *secondary* agents of nature, ever at work to supply the deficiences of the mould in which things were originally cast.   Using the word *deficiencies*, I do not speak with reference to those stronger emotions which a region of mountains is peculiarly fitted to excite.   The bases of those huge barriers may run for a long space in straight lines, and these parallel to each other; the opposite sides of a profound vale may ascend as exact counterparts, or in mutual reflection, like the billows of a troubled sea; and the impression be, from its very simplicity, more awful and sublime.   Sublimity is the result of Nature's first great dealings with the superficies of the earth; but the general tendency of her subsequent operations is towards the production of beauty;

Stickle Tarn, Langdale Pikes from Pavey Ark by
Thomas Allom. 'Under the Precipice . . . lies invisibly Stickle Tarn'.

by a multiplicity of symmetrical parts uniting in a consistent whole. This is every where exemplified along the margins of these lakes. Masses of rock, that have been precipitated from the heights into the area of waters, lie in some places like stranded ships; or have acquired the compact structure of jutting piers; or project in little peninsulas crested with native wood. The smallest rivulet—one whose silent influx is scarcely noticeable in a season of dry weather—so faint is the dimple made by it on the surface of the smooth lake—will be found to have been not useless in shaping, by its deposits of gravel and soil in time of flood, a curve that would not otherwise have existed. But the more powerful brooks, encroaching upon the level of the lake, have, in course of time, given birth to ample promontories of sweeping outline that contrasts boldly with the longitudinal base of the steeps on the opposite shore; while their flat or gently-sloping surfaces never fail to introduce, into the midst of desolation and barrenness, the elements of fertility, even where the habitations of men may not have been raised. These alluvial promontories, however, threaten, in some places, to bisect the waters which they have long adorned; and, in course of ages, they will cause some of the lakes to dwindle into numerous and insignificant pools; which, in their turn, will finally be filled up. But, checking these intrusive calculations, let us rather be content with appearances as they are, and pursue in imagination the meandering shores, whether rugged steeps, admitting of no cultivation, descend into the water; or gently-sloping lawns and woods, or flat and fertile meadows stretch between the margin of the lake and the mountains. Among minuter recommendations will be noticed, especially along bays exposed to the setting-in of strong-winds, the curved rim of fine blue gravel, thrown up in course of time by the waves, half of it perhaps gleaming from under the water, and the corresponding half of a lighter hue; and in other parts bordering the lake, groves, if I may so call them, of reeds and bulrushes; or plots of water-lilies lifting up their large target-shaped leaves to the breeze, while the white flower is heaving upon the wave.

To these may naturally be added the birds that enliven the waters. Wild-ducks in springtime hatch their young in the islands, and upon reedy shores;—the sand-piper, flitting along the stony margins, by its restless note attracts the eye to motions as restless:—upon some jutting rock, or at the edge of a smooth meadow, the stately heron may be descried with folded wings, that might seem to have caught their delicate hue from the blue waters, by the side of which she watches for her sustenance. In winter, the lakes are sometimes resorted to by wild swans; and in that season habitually by widgeons, goldings, and other aquatic fowl of the smaller species. Let me be allowed the aid of verse to describe the evolutions which these visitants sometimes perform, on a fine day towards the close of winter.

> Mark how the feather'd tenants of the flood,
> With grace of motion that might scarcely seem
> Inferior to angelical, prolong
> Their curious pastime! shaping in mid air
> (And sometimes with ambitious wing that soars
> High as the level of the mountain tops,)

A circuit ampler than the lake beneath,
Their own domain;—but ever, while intent
On tracing and retracing that large round,
Their jubilant activity evolves
Hundreds of curves and circlets, to and fro,
Upward and downward, progress intricate
Yet unperplex'd, as if one spirit swayed
Their indefatigable flight.—'Tis done—
Ten times, or more, I fancied it had ceased;
But lo! the vanish'd company again
Ascending;—they approach—I hear their wings
Faint, faint, at first, and then an eager sound
Past in a moment—and as faint again!
They tempt the sun to sport amid their plumes;
They tempt the water or the gleaming ice,
To shew them a fair image;—'tis themselves,
Their own fair forms, upon the glimmering plain,
Painted more soft and fair as they descend
Almost to touch;—then up again aloft,
Up with a sally and a flash of speed,
As if they scorn'd both resting-place and rest!

The ISLANDS, dispersed among these lakes, are neither so numerous nor so beautiful as might be expected from the account that has been given of the manner in which the level areas of the vales are so frequently diversified by rocks, hills, and hillocks, scattered over them; nor are they ornamented (as are several of the lakes in Scotland and Ireland) by the remains of castles or other places of defence; nor with the still more interesting ruins of religious edifices. Every one must regret that scarcely a vestige is left of the Oratory, consecrated to the Virgin, which stood upon Chapel-Holm in Windermere, and that the Chauntry has disappeared, where mass used to be sung, upon St. Herbert's Island, Derwent-water. The islands of the last-mentioned lake are neither fortunately placed nor of pleasing shape; but if the wood upon them were managed with more taste, they might become interesting features in the landscape. There is a beautiful cluster on Winandermere; a pair pleasingly contrasted upon Rydal; nor must the solitary green island of Grasmere be forgotten. In the bosom of each of the lakes of Ennerdale and Devockwater is a single rock, which, owing to its neighbourhood to the sea is—

The haunt of cormorants and sea-mew's clang,

a music well suited to the stern and wild character of the several scenes! It may be worth while here to mention (not as an object of beauty, but of curiosity) that there occasionally appears above the surface of Derwent-water, and always in the same place, a considerable tract of spongy ground covered with aquatic plants, which is called the Floating, but with more propriety might be named the Buoyant, Island; and, on one of the pools near the lake of Esthwaite, may sometimes be seen a mossy Islet, with trees upon it, shifting about before the wind, a lusus naturæ frequent on the great rivers of America, and not unknown in other parts of the world.

fas habeas invisere Tiburis arva,
Albuneæque lacum, atque umbras terrasque natantes.*

This part of the subject may be concluded with observing—that, from the multitude of brooks and torrents that fall into these lakes, and of internal springs by which they are fed, and which circulate through them like veins, they are truly living lakes, "*vivi lacus;*" and are thus discriminated from the stagnant and sullen pools frequent among mountains that have been formed by volcanoes, and from the shallow meres found in flat and fenny countries.   The water is also of crystalline purity; so that, if it were not for the reflections of the incumbent mountains by which it is darkened, a delusion might be felt, by a person resting quietly in a boat on the bosom of Winandermere or Derwent-water, similar to that which Carver so beautifully describes when he was floating alone in the middle of lake Erie or Ontario, and could almost have imagined that his boat was suspended in an element as pure as air, or rather that the air and water were one.

Having spoken of Lakes I must not omit to mention, as a kindred feature of this country, those bodies of still water called TARNS.   In the economy of nature these are useful, as auxiliars to Lakes; for if the whole quantity of water which falls upon the mountains in time of storm were poured down upon the plains without intervention, in some quarters, of such receptacles, the habitable grounds would be much more subject than they are to inundation.   But, as some of the collateral brooks spend their fury, finding a free course toward and also down the channel of the main stream of the vale before those that have to pass through the higher tarns and lakes have filled their several basins, a gradual distribution is effected; and the waters thus reserved, instead of uniting, to spread ravage and deformity, with those which meet with no such detention, contribute to support, for a length of time, the vigour of many streams without a fresh fall of rain.   Tarns are found in some of the vales, and are numerous upon the mountains.   A Tarn, in a *Vale*, implies, for the most part, that the bed of the vale is not happily formed; that the water of the brooks can neither wholly escape, nor diffuse itself over a large area.   Accordingly, in such situations, Tarns are often surrounded by an unsightly tract of boggy ground; but this is not always the case, and in the cultivated parts of the country, when the shores of the Tarn

* See that admirable Idyllium, the Catillus and Salia, of Landor.

Opposite: Afforestation on the screes of Helvellyn near Thirlmere.

Ullswater in winter.

Two views of Keswick Lake by William Westall, 1820. *Above left*: Keswick Lake from Barrow Common. *Above right*: Keswick Lake from the east side. Sara Hutchinson said of these two aquatints, '. . . the view of Keswick from Barrow Common . . . and the Twilight scene . . . are my favourites. Westall tells me that the former has gained him great credit amon[g] the Artists for its execution—and I could not have believed an Engraving could have given the quiet and solemn feeling inspired by such a scene as the latter.' (*The Letters of Sara Hutchinson*, ed. Coburn.)

Sir George Beaumont's favourite picture, 'Landscape with Hagar and the Angel', oil painting by Claude Gellée, called Lorrain. This was one of the four Claudes given by Sir George to the National Gallery in 1826. The little painting ($20\frac{1}{2} \times 16$ in) was his favourite. 'He dealt with it,' said a friend, 'almost as a man might deal with a child he loved. He travelled with it, carried it about with him and valued it beyond any picture which he had.' Wordsworth must often have seen it and discussed it with Sir George. It is typical of the Claudian landscapes which were particularly popular in England, and greatly influenced artists working in the Lakes in Wordsworth's lifetime.

are determined, it differs only from the Lake in being smaller, and in belonging mostly to a smaller valley, or circular recess. Of this class of miniature lakes, Loughrigg Tarn, near Grasmere, is the most beautiful example. It has a margin of green firm meadows, of rocks, and rocky woods, a few reeds here a little company of water-lilies there, with beds of gravel or stone beyond; a tiny stream issuing neither briskly nor sluggishly out of it; but its feeding rills, from the shortness of their course, so small as to be scarcely visible. Five or six cottages are reflected in its peaceful bosom; rocky and barren steeps rise up above the hanging enclosures; and the solemn pikes of Langdale overlook, from a distance, the low cultivated ridge of land that forms the northern boundary of this small, quiet, and fertile domain. The *mountain* Tarns can only be recommended to the notice of the inquisitive traveller who has time to spare. They are difficult of access and naked; yet some of them are, in their permanent forms, very grand; and there are accidents of things which would make the meanest of them interesting. At all events, one of these pools is an acceptable sight to the mountain wanderer; not merely as an incident that diversifies the prospect, but as forming in his mind a centre or conspicuous point to which objects, otherwise disconnected or insubordinated, may be referred. Some few have a varied outline, with bold heath-clad promontories; and, as they mostly lie at the foot of a steep precipice, the water where the sun is not shining upon it, appears black and sullen; and, round the margin, huge stones and masses of rock are scattered; some defying conjecture as to the means by which they came thither; and others obviously fallen from on high—the contribution of ages! A not unpleasing sadness is induced by this perplexity, and these images of decay; while the prospect of a body of pure water unattended with groves and other cheerful rural images by which fresh water is usually accompanied, and unable to give furtherance to the meagre vegetation around it—excites a sense of some repulsive power strongly put forth, and thus deepens the melancholy natural to such scenes. Nor is the feeling of solitude often more forcibly or more solemnly impressed than by the side of one of these mountain pools: though desolate and forbidding, it seems a distinct place to repair to; yet where the visitants must be rare, and there can be no disturbance. Water-fowl flock hither; and the lonely Angler may here be seen; but the imagination, not content with this scanty allowance of society, is tempted to attribute a voluntary power to every change which takes place in such a spot, whether it be the breeze that wanders over the surface of the water, or the splendid lights of evening resting upon it in the midst of awful precipices.

> There, sometimes does a leaping fish
> Send through the tarn a lonely cheer;
> The crags repeat the raven's croak
> In symphony austere:
> Thither the rainbow comes, the cloud,
> And mists that spread the flying shroud,
> And sunbeams, and the sounding blast.

It will be observed that this country is bounded on the south and east by the sea, which combines beautifully, from many elevated points, with the inland scenery; and from the bay of Morcamb, the sloping shores and background of distant mountains are seen, composing pictures equally distinguished for amenity and grandeur. But the æstuaries on this coast are in a great measure bare at low water*; and there is no instance of the sea running far up among the mountains, and mingling with the Lakes, which are such in the strict and usual sense of the word, being of fresh water. Nor have the streams, from the shortness of their course, time to acquire that body of water necessary to confer upon them much majesty. In fact, the most considerable, while they continue in the mountain and lake-country, are rather large brooks than rivers. The water is perfectly pellucid, through which in many places are seen, to a great depth, their beds of rock, or of blue gravel, which give to the water itself an exquisitely cerulean colour: this is

---

* In fact there is not an instance of a harbour on the Cumberland side of the Solway frith that is not dry at low water; that of Ravenglass, at the mouth of the Esk, as a natural harbour is much the best. The Sea appears to have been retiring slowly for ages from this coast. From Whitehaven to St. Bees extends a track of level ground, about five miles in length, which formerly must have been under salt water, so as to have made an island of the high ground that stretches between it and the Sea.

Two views from the Langdale Pikes, by Thomas Allom.
Above: Looking over the head of Langdale to Bowfell. Allom was an
indefatigable topographical illustrator, 'Fearless of danger, patient of fatigue, he
roamed round the Lake District . . . through all the alterations of storm,
sunshine, wind and rain . . .' (Introduction to Rose's *Westmorland, Cumberland
. . . Illustrated*, for which Allom supplied about eighty views of the Lake
District. Wordsworth's copy of this book is still at Grasmere.)

Opposite: Looking south-east over Windermere.

particularly striking in the rivers Derwent and Duddon, which may be
compared, such and so various are their beauties, to any two rivers of equal
length of course in any country. The number of the torrents and smaller
brooks is infinite, with their water-falls and water-breaks; and they need not
here be described. I will only observe that, as many, even of the smallest
rills, have either found, or made for themselves, recesses in the sides of the
mountains or in the vales, they have tempted the primitive inhabitants to
settle near them for shelter; and hence, cottages so placed, by seeming to
withdraw from the eye, are the more endeared to the feelings.

The WOODS consist chiefly of oak, ash, and birch, and here and there
Wych-elm, with underwood of hazle, the white and black thorn, and hollies;
in moist places alders and willows abound; and yews among the
rocks. Formerly the whole country must have been covered with wood to a

great height up the mountains; where native Scotch firs* must have grown in great profusion, as they do in the northern part of Scotland to this day. But not one of these old inhabitants has existed, perhaps for some hundreds of years; the beautiful traces, however, of the universal sylvan† appearance the country formerly had, yet survive in the native coppice-woods that have been protected by inclosures, and also in the forest-trees and hollies, which, though disappearing fast, are yet scattered both over the inclosed and uninclosed parts of the mountains. The same is expressed by the beauty and intricacy with which the fields and coppice-woods are often intermingled: the plough of the first settlers having followed naturally the veins of richer, dryer, or less stony soil; and thus it has shaped out an intermixture of wood and lawn, with a grace and wildness, which it would have been impossible for the hand of studied art to produce. Other trees have been introduced within these last fifty years, such as beeches, larches, limes, &c. and plantations of firs, seldom with advantage, and often with great injury to the appearance of the country; but the sycamore (which I believe was brought into this island from Germany, not more than two hundred years ago) has long been the favourite of the cottagers; and, with the fir, has been chosen to screen their dwellings: and is sometimes found in the fields whither the winds or the waters may have carried its seeds.

The want most felt, however, is that of timber trees. There are a few *magnificent* ones to be found near any of the lakes; and unless greater care be taken, there will, in a short time, scarcely be left an ancient oak that would repay the cost of felling. The neighbourhood of Rydal, notwithstanding the havoc which has been made, is yet nobly distinguished. In the woods of Lowther, also, is found an almost matchless store of ancient trees, and the majesty and wildness of their native forest.

Among the smaller vegetable ornaments must be reckoned the bilberry, a ground plant, never so beautiful as in early spring, when it is seen under bare or budding trees that imperfectly intercept the sun-shine, covering the rocky knolls with a pure mantle of fresh verdure, more lively than the herbage of the open fields;—the broom that spreads luxuriantly along rough pastures, and in the month of June interveins the steep copses with its golden blossoms;— and the juniper, a rich evergreen, that thrives in spite of cattle, upon the uninclosed parts of the mountains:—the Dutch myrtle diffuses fragrance in moist places; and there is an endless variety of brilliant flowers in the fields and meadows, which, if the agriculture of the country were more carefully attended to, would disappear. Nor can I omit again to notice the lichens and mosses: their profusion, beauty, and variety, exceed those of any other country I have seen.

---

* This species of fir is in character much superior to the American which has usurped its place: Where the fir is planted for ornament, let it be by all means of the aboriginal species, which can only be procured from the Scotch nurseries.

---

† A squirrel (so I have heard the old people of Wytheburn say) might have gone from their chapel to Keswick without alighting on the ground.

The lonely angler on Sty Head Tarn, pencil and wash drawing. A leaf from the
sketch-book of an unidentified artist touring in the Lakes in about 1825, 'and the
lonely Angler may here be seen'.

It may now be proper to say a few words respecting climate, and "skiey
influences," in which this region, as far as the character of its landscapes is
affected by them, may, upon the whole, be considered fortunate. The
country is, indeed, subject to much bad weather, and it has been ascertained
that twice as much rain falls here as in many parts of the island; but the
number of black drizzling days, that blot out the face of things, is by no means
proportionally great. Nor is a continuance of thick, flagging, damp air, so
common as in the West of England and Ireland. The rain here comes down
heartily, and is frequently succeeded by clear, bright weather, when every
brook is vocal, and every torrent sonorous; brooks and torrents, which are
never muddy, even in the heaviest floods, except, after a drought, they
happen to be defiled for a short time by waters that have swept along dusty
roads, or have broken out into ploughed fields. Days of unsettled weather,
with partial showers, are very frequent; but the showers, darkening, or
brightning, as they fly from hill to hill, are not less grateful to the eye than
finely interwoven passages of gay and sad music are touching to the
ear. Vapours exhaling from the lakes and meadows after sun-rise, in a hot
season, or, in moist weather, brooding upon the heights, or descending
towards the valleys with inaudible motion, give a visionary character to
everything around them; and are in themselves so beautiful, as to dispose us
to enter into the feelings of those simple nations (such as the Laplanders of
this day) by whom they are taken for guardian deities of the mountains; or to
sympathise with others who have fancied these delicate apparitions to be the

Colwith Force, 1837, pencil and chalk drawing by Edward Lear.

spirits of their departed ancestors.   Akin to these are fleecy clouds resting upon the hill-tops; they are not easily managed in picture, with their accompaniments of blue sky; but how glorious are they in nature! how pregnant with imagination for the poet! and the height of the Cumbrian mountains is sufficient to exhibit daily and hourly instances of those mysterious attachments.   Such clouds, cleaving to their stations, or lifting up suddenly their glittering heads from behind rocky barriers, or hurrying out of sight with speed of the sharpest edge— will often tempt an inhabitant to congratulate himself on belonging to a country of mists and clouds and storms, and make him think of the blank sky of Egypt, and of the cerulean vacancy of Italy, as an unanimated and even a sad spectacle. The atmosphere, however, as in every county subject to much rain, is frequently unfavourable to landscape, especially when keen winds succeed the rain which are apt to produce coldness, spottiness, and an unmeaning or repulsive detail in the distance;—a sunless frost, under a canopy of leaden and shapeless clouds, is, as far as it allows things to be seen, equally disagreeable.

It has been said that in human life there are moments worth ages. In a more subdued tone of sympathy may we affirm, that in the climate of England there are, for the lover of nature, days which are worth whole months,—I might say—even years. One of these favoured days sometimes occurs in spring-time, when the soft air is breathing over the blossoms and new-born verdure, which inspired Buchanan with his beautiful Ode to the first of May; the air, which, in the luxuriance of his fancy, he likens to that of the golden age,—to that which gives motion to the funereal cypresses on the banks of Lethe;—to the air which is to salute beatified spirits when expiatory fires shall have consumed the earth with all her habitations. But it is in autumn that days of such affecting influence most frequently intervene;—the atmosphere seems refined, and the sky rendered more crystalline, as the vivifying heat of the year abates; the lights and shadows are more delicate; the coloring is richer and more finely harmonized; and, in this season of stillness, the ear being unoccupied, or only gently excited, the sense of vision becomes more susceptible of its appropriate enjoyments. A resident in a country like this which we are treating of, will agree with me, that the presence of a lake is indispensable to exhibit in perfection the beauty of one of these days; and he must have experienced, while looking on the unruffled waters, that the imagination, by their aid, is carried into recesses of feeling otherwise impenetrable. The reason of this is, that the heavens are not only brought down into the bosom of the earth, but that the earth is mainly looked at, and thought of, through the medium of a purer element. The happiest time is when the equinoxial gales are departed; but their fury may probably be called to mind by the sight of a few shattered boughs, whose leaves do not differ in colour from the faded foliage of the stately oaks from which these relics of the storm depend: all else speaks of tranquillity;—not a breath of air, no restlessness of insects, and not a moving object perceptible—except the clouds gliding in the depths of the lake, or the traveller passing along, an inverted image, whose motion seems governed by the quiet of a time, to which its archetype, the living person, is, perhaps, insensible:—or it may happen, that the figure of one of the larger birds, a raven or a heron, is crossing silently among the reflected clouds, while the voice of the real bird, from the element aloft, gently awakens in the spectator the recollection of appetites and instincts, pursuits and occupations, that deform and agitate the world,—yet have no power to prevent nature from putting on an aspect capable of satisfying the most intense cravings for the tranquil, the lovely, and the perfect, to which man, the noblest of her creatures, is subject.

Thus far, of climate, as influencing the feelings through its effect on the objects of sense. We may add, that whatever has been said upon the advantages derived to these scenes from a changeable atmosphere, would apply, perhaps still more forcibly, to their appearance under the varied solemnities of night. Milton, it will be remembered, has given a *clouded* moon to Paradise itself. In the night-season also, the narrowness of the vales, and comparative smallness of the lakes, are especially adapted to bring surrounding objects home to the eye and to the heart. The stars, taking their stations above the hill-tops, are contemplated from a spot like the Abyssinian recess of Rasselas, with much more touching interest than they are likely to excite when looked at from an open country with ordinary undulations: and it must be obvious, that it is the *bays* only of large lakes that can present such contrasts of light and shadow as those of smaller dimensions display from every quarter. A deep contracted valley, with diffused waters, such a valley and plains level and wide as those of Chaldea, are the two extremes in which the beauty of the heavens and their connexion with the earth are most sensibly felt. Nor do the advantages I have been speaking of imply here an exclusion of the aerial effects of distance. These are insured by the height of the mountains, and are found, even in the narrowest of vales, where they lengthen in perspective, or act (if the expression may be used) as telescopes for the open country.

The subject would bear to be enlarged upon: but I will conclude this section with a night-scene suggested by the Vale of Keswick. The Fragment is well known; but it gratifies me to insert it, as the Writer was one of the first who led the way to a worthy admiration of this country.

> Now sunk the sun, now twilight sunk, and night
> Rode in her zenith; not a passing breeze
> Sigh'd to the grove, which in the midnight air
> Stood motionless, and in the peaceful floods
> Inverted hung: for now the billows slept
> Along the shore, nor heav'd the deep; but spread
> A shining mirror to the moon's pale orb,
> Which, dim and waning, o'er the shadowy cliffs,
> The solemn woods, and spiry mountain tops,
> Her glimmering faintness threw: now every eye,
> Oppress'd with toil, was drown'd in deep repose,
> Save that the unseen Shepherd in his watch,
> Propp'd on his crook, stood listening by the fold,
> And gaz'd the starry vault, and pendant moon;
> Nor voice, nor sound, broke on the deep serene;
> But the soft murmur of swift-gushing rills,
> Forth issuing from the mountain's distant steep.
> (Unheard till now, and now scarce heard) proclaim'd
> All things at rest, and imag'd the still voice
> Of quiet, whispering in the ear of night.*

* Dr. Brown, the author of this fragment, was from his infancy brought up in Cumberland, and should have remembered that the practice of folding sheep by night is unknown among these mountains, and that the image of the Shepherd upon the watch is out of its place, and belongs only to countries, with a warmer climate, that are subject to ravages from beasts of prey. It is pleasing to notice a dawn of imaginative feeling in these verses. Tickel, a man of no common genius, chose, for the subject of a Poem, Kensington Gardens, in preference to the Banks of the Derwent, within a mile or two of which he was born. But this was in the reign of Queene Anne, or George the first. Progress must have been made in the interval; though the traces of it, except in the works of Thomson and Dyer, are not very obvious.

SECTION SECOND

ASPECT OF THE COUNTRY AS AFFECTED BY ITS INHABITANTS

HITHERTO I have chiefly spoken of the features by which nature has discriminated this country from others. I will now describe, in general terms, in what manner it is indebted to the hand of man. What I have to notice on this subject will emanate most easily and perspicuously from a description of the ancient and present inhabitants, their occupations, their condition of life, the distribution of landed property among them, and the tenure by which it is holden.

The reader will suffer me here to recall to his mind the shapes of the vallies, and their position with respect to each other, and the forms and substance of the intervening mountains. He will people the vallies with lakes and rivers: the coves and sides of the mountain with pools and torrents; and will bound half of the circle which we have contemplated by the sands of the sea, or by the sea itself. He will conceive that, from the point upon which he stood, he looks down upon this scene before the country had been penetrated by any inhabitants:—to vary his sensations, and to break in upon their stillness, he will form to himself an image of the tides visiting and re-visiting the friths, the main sea dashing against the bolder shore, the rivers pursuing their course to be lost in the mighty mass of waters. He may see or hear in fancy the winds sweeping over the lakes, or piping with a loud voice among the mountain peaks; and, lastly, may think of the primeval woods shedding and renewing their leaves with no human eye to notice, or human heart to regret or welcome the change. "When the first settlers entered this region (says an animated writer) they found it overspread with wood; forest trees, the fir, the oak, the ash, and the birch had skirted the fells, tufted the hills, and shaded the vallies, through centuries of silent solitude; the birds and beasts of prey reigned over the meeker species; and the *bellum inter omnia* maintained the balance of nature in the empire of beasts."

Such was the state and appearance of this region when the aboriginal colonists of the Celtic tribes were first driven or drawn towards it, and became joint tenants with the wolf, the boar, the wild bull, the red deer, and the leigh, a gigantic species of deer which has been long extinct; while the inaccessible crags were occupied by the falcon, the raven, and the eagle. The inner parts were too secluded, and of too little value, to participate much of the benefit of Roman manners; and though these

'A view of Darwentwater &c. from Crow-Park' by Thomas Smith of Derby.
Smith was in Keswick at about the same time as William Bellers, *c.* 1752, but his
print of Derwentwater did not come out until 1761. It combines the elements of
Beauty, Horror and Immensity with an unusual strain of fantasy which finds no
echo in the works of Wordsworth.

conquerors encouraged the Britons to the improvement of their lands in the plain country of Furness and Cumberland, they seem to have had little connexion with the mountains, except for military purposes, or in subservience to the profit they drew from the mines.

When the Romans retired from Great Britain, it is well known that these mountain-fastnesses furnished a protection to some unsubdued Britons, long after the more accessible and more fertile districts had been seized by the Saxon or Danish invader. A few, though distinct, traces of Roman forts or camps, as at Ambleside, and upon Dunmallet, and a few circles of rude stones attributed to the Druids,* are the only vestiges that remain upon the surface of the country, of these ancient occupants; and, as the Saxons and Danes, who succeeded to the possession of the villages and hamlets which had been established by the Britons, seem at first to have confined themselves to the open country,—we may descend at once to times long posterior to the conquest by the Normans, when their feudal polity was regularly established. We may easily conceive that these narrow dales and mountain sides, choaked up as they must have been with wood, lying out of the way of communication with other parts of the Island, and upon the edge of a hostile

---

* It is not improbable that these circles were once numerous, and that many of them may yet endure in a perfect state, under no very deep covering of soil. A friend of the Author, while making a trench in a level piece of ground, not far from the banks of the Emont, but in no connection with that river, met with some stones which seemed to him formally arranged; this excited his curiosity, and proceeding, he uncovered a perfect circle of stones, from two to three or four feet high, with a *sanctum sanctorum*,—the whole a complete place of Druidical worship of small dimensions, having the same sort of relation to Stonehenge, Long Meg and her Daughters near the river Eden, and Karl Lofts near Shap (if this last be not Danish), that a rural chapel bears to a stately church, or to one of our noble cathedrals. This interesting little monument having passed, with the field in which it was found, into other hands, has been destroyed. It is much regretted, that the striking relic of antiquity at Shap has been in a great measure destroyed also.

The DAUGHTERS of LONG MEG are placed not in an oblong, as the STONES of SHAP, but in a perfect circle, eighty yards in diameter, and seventy-two in number, and from above three yards high, to less than so many feet: a little way out of the circle stands LONG MEG herself—a single stone eighteen feet high.

When the Author first saw this monument, he came upon it by surprize, therefore might over-rate its importance as an object; but he must say, that though it is not to be compared with Stonehenge, he has not seen any other remains of those dark ages, which can pretend to rival it in singularity and dignity of appearance.

> A weight of awe not easy to be borne
> Fell suddenly upon my spirit, cast
> From the dread bosom of the unknown past,
> When first I saw that sisterhood forlorn;—
> And Her, whose strength and stature seem to scorn
> The power of years—pre-eminent, and placed
> Apart, to overlook the circle vast.
> Speak, Giant-mother! tell it to the Morn,
> While she dispels the cumbrous shades of night;
> Let the Moon hear, emerging from a cloud,
> When, how, and wherefore, rose on British ground
> That wondrous Monument, whose mystic round
> Forth shadows, some have deemed, to mortal sight
> The inviolable God that tames the proud.

The Druidical Circle near Keswick, Castlerigg, close to the
Ambleside–Keswick road, 'one of those circles of upright stones, large and
perfect, which we are accustomed to call Druid Temples', by J. B. Pyne.

kingdom, could have little attraction for the high-born and powerful;
especially as the more open parts of the country furnished positions for
castles and houses of defence, sufficient to repel any of those sudden attacks,
which, in the then rude state of military knowledge, could be made upon
them. Accordingly, the more retired regions (and to such I am now
confining myself) must have been neglected or shunned even by the persons
whose baronial or signioral rights extended over them, and left, doubtless,
partly as a place of refuge for outlaws and robbers, and partly granted out for
the more settled habitation of a few vassals following the employment of
shepherds or woodlanders. Hence these lakes and inner vallies are un-
adorned by any remains of ancient grandeur, castles, or monastic edifices,
which are only found upon the skirts of the country, as Furness Abbey,
Calder Abbey, the Priory of Lannercost, Gleaston Castle,—long ago a
residence of the Flemings,—and the numerous ancient castles of the
Cliffords, the Lucys, and the Dacres. On the southern side of these
mountains, (especially in that part known by the name of Furness Fells,
which is more remote from the borders,) the state of society would
necessarily be more settled; though it also was fashioned, not a little, by its
neighbourhood to a hostile kingdom. We will, therefore, give a sketch of

the economy of the Abbots in the distribution of lands among their tenants, as similar plans were doubtless adopted by other Lords, and as the consequences have affected the face of the country materially to the present day, being, in fact, one of the principal causes which give it such a striking superiority, in beauty and interest, over all other parts of the island.

"When the Abbots of Furness," says an author before cited, "enfranchised their villains, and raised them to the dignity of customary tenants, the lands, which they had cultivated for their lord, were divided into whole tenements; each of which, besides the customary annual rent, was charged with the obligation of having in readiness a man completely armed for the king's service on the borders, or elsewhere; each of these whole tenements was again subdivided into four equal parts; each villain had one; and the party tenant contributed his share to the support of the man of arms, and of other burdens.   These divisions were not properly distinguished; the land remained mixed; each tenant had a share through all the arable and meadow-land, and common pasture over all the wastes.   These sub-tenements were judged sufficient for the support of so many families; and no further division was permitted.   These divisions and sub-divisions were convenient at the time for which they were calculated: the land, so parcelled out, was, of necessity more attended to, and the industry greater, when more persons were to be supported by the produce of it.   The frontier of the kingdom, within which Furness was considered, was in a constant state of attack and defence; more hands therefore, were necessary to guard the coast, to repel an invasion from Scotland, or make reprisals on the hostile neighbour.   The dividing the lands in such manner as has been shown, increased the number of inhabitants, and kept them at home till called for: and, the land being mixed, and the several tenants united in equipping the plough, the absence of the fourth man was no prejudice to the cultivation of his land, which was committed to the care of three.

While the villains of Low Furness were thus distributed over the land, and employed in agriculture; those of High Furness were charged with the care of flocks and herds, to protect them from the wolves which lurked in the thickets, and in winter to browze them with the tender sprouts of hollies and ash.   This custom was not till lately discontinued in High Furness; and holly-trees were carefully preserved for that purpose when all other wood was cleared off; large tracts of common being so covered with these trees, as to have the appearance of a forest of hollies.   At the Shepherd's call, the flocks surrounded the holly-bush, and received the croppings at his hand, which they greedily nibbled up, bleating for more.   The Abbots of Furness enfranchised these pastoral vassals, and permitted them to enclose *quillets* to their houses, for which they paid encroachment rent."—West's *Antiquities of Furness*.

However desirable, for the purposes of defence, a numerous population might be, it was not possible to make at once the same numerous allotments among the untilled vallies, and upon the sides of the mountains, as had been made in the cultivated plains.   The enfranchised shepherd, or woodlander, having chosen there his place of residence, builds it of sods, or of the mountain-stone, and, with the permission of his lord, encloses, like

Robinson Crusoe, a small croft or two immediately at his door for such animals as he wishes to protect. Others are happy to imitate his example, and avail themselves of the same privileges: and thus a population, mainly of Danish or Norse origin, as the dialect indicates, crept on towards the more secluded parts of the vallies. Chapels, daughters of some distant mother church, are first erected in the more open and fertile vales, as those of Bowness and Grasmere, offsets of Kendal: which again, after a period as the settled population increases, become mother-churches to smaller edifices, planted, at length, in almost every dale throughout the country. The inclosures, formed by the tenantry, are for a long time confined to the home-steads; and the arable and meadow land of the vales is possessed in common field; the several portions being marked out by stones, bushes, or trees: which portions, where the custom has survived, to this day are called *dales*, from the word *deylen*, to distribute; but, while the valley was thus lying open, enclosures seem to have taken place upon the sides of the mountains; because the land there was not intermixed, and was of little comparative value; and, therefore, small opposition would be made to its being appropriated by those to whose habitations it was contiguous. Hence the singular appearance which the sides of many of the mountains exhibit, intersected, as they are, almost to the summit, with stone walls. When first erected, these stone fences must have little disfigured the face of the country; as part of the lines would every where be hidden by the quantity of native wood then remaining; and the lines would also be broken (as they still are) by the rocks which interrupt and vary their course. In the meadows, and in those parts of the lower grounds where the soil has not been sufficiently drained, and could not afford a stable foundation, there, when the increasing value of land, and the inconvenience suffered from intermixed plots of ground in common field, had induced each inhabitant to enclose his own, they were compelled to make the fences of alders, willows, and other trees. These, where the native wood had disappeared, have frequently enriched the vallies with a sylvan appearance; while the intricate intermixture of property has given to the fences a graceful irregularity, which, where large properties are prevalent, and large capitals employed in agriculture, is unknown. This sylvan appearance is heightened by the number of ash-trees planted in rows along the quick fences, and along the walls, for the purpose of browzing the cattle at the approach of winter. The branches are lopped off and strewn upon the pastures; and when the cattle have stripped them of the leaves, they are used for repairing the hedges or for fuel.

We have thus seen a numerous body of Dalesmen creeping into possession of their home-steads, their little crofts, their mountain-enclosures; and, finally, the whole vale is visibly divided; except, perhaps, here and there some marshy ground, which, till fully drained, would not repay the trouble of enclosing. But these last partitions do not seem to have been general, till long after the pacification of the Borders, by the union of the two crowns: when the cause, which had first determined the distribution of land into such small parcels, had not only ceased,—but likewise a general improvement had taken place in the country, with a correspondent rise in the value of its produce. From the time of the union, it is certain that this

Stockley Bridge in 1814, by William Green. A typical pack-horse bridge at the head of Borrowdale, carrying the track to Wastdale by Sty Head. Wordsworth comments on these structures which are 'in themselves models of elegance, as if they had been formed upon principles of the most thoughtful architecture.'

species of feudal population must rapidly have diminished. That it was formerly much more numerous than it is at present, is evident from the multitude of tenements (I do not mean houses, but small divisions of land) which belonged formerly each to a several proprietor, and for which separate fines are paid to the manorial lord at this day. These are often in the proportion of four to one of the present occupants. "Sir Launcelot Threlkeld, who lived in the reign of Henry VII., was wont to say, he had three noble houses, one for pleasure, Crosby, in Westmorland, where he had a park full of deer; one for profit and warmth, wherein to reside in winter, namely, Yanwith, nigh Penrith; and the third, Threlkeld, (on the edge of the vale of Keswick), well stocked with tenants to go with him to the wars." But, as I have said, from the union of the two crowns, this numerous vassalage (their services not being wanted) would rapidly diminish; various tenements would be united in one possessor; and the aboriginal houses, probably little better than hovels, like the kraels of savages, or the huts of the Highlanders of Scotland, would fall into decay, and the places of many be supplied by substantial and comfortable buildings, a majority of which remain to this day scattered over the vallies, and are often the only dwellings found in them.

From the time of the erection of these houses, till within the last sixty years, the state of society, though no doubt slowly and gradually improving, underwent no material change. Corn was grown in these vales (through which no carriage-road had yet been made) sufficient upon each estate to furnish bread for each family, and no more; notwithstanding the union of several tenements, the possessions of each inhabitant still being small, in the same field was seen an intermixture of different crops; and the plough was interrupted by little rocks, mostly overgrown with wood, or by spongy places, which the tiller of the soil had neither leisure nor capital to convert into firm land. The storms and moisture of the climate induced them to sprinkle their upland property with outhouses of native stone, as places of shelter for their sheep, where, in tempestuous weather, food was distributed to them. Every family spun from its own flock the wool with which it was clothed; a weaver was here and there found among them; and the rest of their wants was supplied by the produce of the yarn, which they carded and spun in their own houses, and carried to market, either under their arms, or more frequently on pack-horses, a small train taking their way weekly down the valley or over the mountains to the most commodious town. They had, as I have said, their rural chapel, and of course their minister, in clothing or in manner of life, in no respect differing from themselves, except on the Sabbath-day; this was the sole distinguished individual among them; every thing else, person and possession, exhibited a perfect equality, a community of shepherds and agriculturists, proprietors, for the most part, of the lands which they occupied and cultivated.

While the process above detailed was going on, the native forest must have been every where receding; but trees were planted for the sustenance of the flocks in winter,—such was then the rude state of agriculture; and, for the same cause, it was necessary that care should be taken of some part of the growth of the native woods. Accordingly, in Queen Elizabeth's time, this

Opposite above: A watercolour view of Windermere showing Brathay Hall and the Langdale Pikes, 1810, by John Harden, who leased Brathay Hall from 1804 to 1833. When it was built in 1789 Coleridge said of it, 'Amid these awful mountains Mr Law has built a white palace at the head of Winandermere, with his twenty cropped trees, four stumps standing upon the trunk of each, all looking like strange Devils with perpendicular horns.' The Hardens entertained many artists at Brathay Hall, and it was there that Wordsworth met Constable in 1806.

Opposite below: Clappersgate, Brathay River, 1810, by John Harden. From the slate wharf at the foot of the Brathay, close to Harden's house, the fine slates quarried in Langdale were transported down Windermere. The scene recalls a passage from the *Guide*—'The water is also of Crystalline purity: so that if it were not for the reflections of the incumbent mountains by which it is darkened, a delusion might be felt, by a person resting quietly in a boat on the bosom of Winandermere . . . that his boat was suspended in an element as pure as air, or rather that the air and water were one.'

Harter Fell at the
headwater of Haweswater
Reservoir.

Lilley of the Valley Island on Windermere, a watercolour by John Harden. Wordsworth said in *The Prelude*, 'a sister Isle/Beneath the oaks' umbrageous covert, sown/With lilies of the valley, like a field.'

Old Miller Bridge, Ambleside, 1843, a watercolour by John Harden. This bridge over the River Rothay, not far from Rydal Mount, made of timber supported on stone piers, is characteristic of the Lake District.

was so strongly felt, that a petition was made to the Crown, praying, "that the Blomaries in High Furness might be abolished, on account of the quantity of wood which was consumed in them for the use of the mines, to the great detriment of the cattle."   But this same cause, about a hundred years after, produced   effects   directly   contrary   to   those   which   had   been deprecated.   The re-establishment, at that period, of furnaces upon a large scale, made it the interest of the people to convert the steeper and more stony of the enclosures, sprinkled over with remains of the native forest, into close woods, which, when cattle and sheep were excluded, rapidly sowed and thickened themselves.   The reader's attention has been directed to the cause by which tufts of wood, pasturage, meadow, and arable land, with its various produce, are intricately intermingled in the same field; and he will now see, in like manner, how enclosures entirely of wood, and those of cultivated ground, are blended all over the country under a law of similar wildness.

An historic detail has thus been given of the manner in which the hand of man has acted upon the surface of the inner regions of this mountainous country, as incorporated with and subservient to the powers and processes of nature.   We will now take a view of the same agency—acting, within narrower bounds, for the production of the few works of art and accommodations of life which, in so simple a state of society, could be necessary.   These are merely habitations of man and coverts for beasts, roads and bridges, and places of worship.

And to begin with the COTTAGES.   They are scattered over the vallies, and under the hill sides, and on the rocks; and, even to this day, in the more retired dales, without any intrusion of more assuming buildings;

> Cluster'd like stars some few, but single most,
> And lurking dimly in their shy retreats,
> Or glancing on each other cheerful looks,
> Like separated stars with clouds between.   MS.

The dwelling-houses, and contiguous out-houses, are, in many instances, of the colour of the native rock, out of which they have been built; but, frequently the Dwelling or Fire-house, as it is ordinarily called, has been distinguished from the barn or byer by rough-cast and white wash, which, as the inhabitants are not hasty in renewing it, in a few years acquires, by the influence of weather, a tint at once sober and variegated.   As these houses have been, from father to son, inhabited by persons engaged in the same occupations, yet necessarily with changes in their circumstances, they have received without incongruity additions and accommodations adapted to the needs of each successive occupant, who, being for the most part proprietor, was at liberty to follow his own fancy: so that these humble dwellings remind the contemplative spectator of a production of nature, and may (using a strong expression) rather be said to have grown than to have been erected;— to have risen, by an instinct of their own, out of the native rock—so little is there in them of formality, such is their wildness and beauty.   Among the numerous recesses and projections in the walls and in the different stages of their roofs, are seen bold and harmonious effects of contrasted sunshine and

Farmhouse at Glencoin, Ullswater, by William Green.
'Nor will the singular beauty of the chimneys escape the eye of the attentive
traveller.' Canon Rawnsley in *Wordsworthiana : Reminiscences of Wordsworth*
recalls a local mason saying, 'Wudsworth was a great un for chimleys . . . And
he'ed a great fancy an 'aw for chimleys square up hauf way, and round the
t'other. And so we built 'em that how.'

shadow.   It is a favourable circumstance, that the strong winds which sweep
down the vallies, induced the inhabitants, at a time when the materials for
building were easily procured, to furnish many of these dwellings with
substantial porches; and such as have not this defence, are seldom
unprovided with a projection of two large slates over their thresholds.   Nor
will the singular beauty of the chimneys escape the eye of the attentive
traveller.   Sometimes a low chimney, almost upon a level with the roof, is
overlaid with a slate, supported upon four slender pillars, to prevent the wind
from driving the smoke down the chimney.   Others are of a quadrangular
shape, rising one or two feet above the roof: which low square is often
surmounted by a tall cylinder, giving to the cottage chimney the most
beautiful shape in which it is ever seen.   Nor will it be too fanciful or refined
to remark, that there is a pleasing harmony between a tall chimney of this
circular form, and the living column of smoke, ascending from it through the
still air.   These dwellings, mostly built, as has been said, of rough unhewn
stone, are roofed with slates, which were rudely taken from the quarry before

106

the present art of splitting them was understood, and are, therefore, rough and uneven in their surface, so that both the coverings and sides of the houses have furnished places of rest for the seeds of lichens, mosses, ferns, and flowers. Hence buildings, which in their very form call to mind the processes of nature, do thus, clothed in part with a vegetable garb, appear to

Eskdale by George Pickering.
The view shows one of those 'obtrusive . . . large
tracts of Larch-plantations that are overrunning
the hill-sides'. Scawfell, the highest summit
in England, is in shadow on the left.

be received into the bosom of the living principle of things, as it acts and exists among the woods and fields; and, by their colour and their shape, affectingly direct the thoughts to that tranquil course of nature and simplicity, along which the humble-minded inhabitants have, through so many generations, been led. Add the little garden with its shed for bee-hives, its small bed of pot-herbs, and its borders and patches of flowers for Sunday posies, with sometimes a choice of few too much prized to be plucked; an orchard of proportioned size; a cheese-press, often supported by some tree near the door; a cluster of embowering sycamores for summer shade; with a tall fir, through which the winds sing when other trees are leafless; the little rill or household spout murmuring in all seasons;— combine these incidents and images together, and you have the representative idea of a mountain-cottage in this country so beautifully formed in itself, and so richly adorned by the hand of nature.

Till within the last sixty years there was no communication between any of these vales by carriage-roads; all bulky articles were transported on pack-horses. Owing, however, to the population not being concentrated in villages, but scattered, the vallies themselves were intersected as now by innumerable lanes and path-ways leading from house to house and from field to field. These lanes, where they are fenced by stone walls, are mostly bordered with ashes, hazels, wild roses, and beds of tall fern, at their base; while the walls themselves, if old, are overspread with mosses, small ferns, wild strawberries, the geranium, and lichens: and, if the wall happen to rest against a bank of earth, it is sometimes almost wholly concealed by a rich facing of stone-fern. It is a great advantage to a traveller or resident, that these numerous lanes and paths, if he be a zealous admirer of nature, will lead him on into all the recesses of the country, so that the hidden treasures of its landscapes may, by an ever-ready guide, be laid open to his eyes.

Likewise to the smallness of the several properties is owing the great number of bridges over the brooks and torrents, and the daring and graceful neglect of danger or accommodation with which so many of them are constructed, the rudeness of the forms of some, and their endless variety. But, when I speak of this rudeness, I must at the same time add, that many of these structures are in themselves models of elegance, as if they had been formed upon principles of the most thoughtful architecture. It is to be regretted that these monuments of the skill of our ancestors, and of that happy instinct by which consummate beauty was produced, are disappearing fast; but sufficient specimens remain* to give a high gratification to the man of genuine taste. Travellers who may not have been accustomed to pay attention to things so inobtrusive, will excuse me if I point out the proportion between the span and elevation of the arch, the lightness of the parapet, and the graceful manner in which its curve follows faithfully that of the arch.

Upon this subject I have nothing further to notice, except the PLACES OF WORSHIP, which have mostly a little school-house adjoining.† The architecture of these churches and chapels, where they have not been recently

---

* Written some time ago. The injury done since, is more than could have been calculated upon.

Singula de nobis anni prædantur euntes. This is in the the course of things; but why should the genius that directed the ancient architecture of these vales have deserted them? For the bridges, churches, mansions, cottages, and their richly fringed and flat-roofed outhouses, venerable as the grange of some old abbey, have been substituted structures, in which baldness only seems to have been studied, or plans of the most vulgar utility. But some improvement may be looked for in future; the gentry *recently* have copied the old models, and successful instances might be pointed out, if I could take the liberty.

† In some places scholars were formerly taught in the church, and at others the school-house was a sort of anti-chapel to the place of worship, being under the same roof; an arrangement which was abandoned as irreverent. It continues, however, to this day in Borrowdale. In the parish register of that chapelry is a notice, that a youth who had quitted the valley, and died in one of the towns on the coast of Cumberland, had requested that his body should be brought and interred at the foot of the pillar by which he had been accustomed to sit while a school-boy. One cannot but regret that parish registers so seldom contain any thing but bare names; in a few of this country, especially in that of Loweswater, I have found interesting notices of unusual natural occurrences—characters of the deceased, and particulars of their lives. There is no good reason why such memorials should not be frequent; these short and simple annals would in future ages become precious.

Mill Beck and Buttermere Chapel by George Pickering.
'A man must be very insensible who could not be touched with pleasure by the
sight of the chapel of Buttermere, so strikingly expressing
by its diminutive size . . . how small must be the congregation assembled
as it were like one family.'

rebuilt or modernised, is of a style not less appropriate and admirable than
that of the dwelling-houses and other structures. How sacred the spirit by
which our forefathers were directed! The *religio loci* is no where violated by
these unstinted, yet unpretending, works of human hands. They exhibit
generally a well-proportioned oblong, with a suitable porch, in some
instances a steeple tower, and in others nothing more than a small belfry, in
which one or two bells hang visibly. But these objects, though pleasing in
their forms, must necessarily, more than others in rural scenery, derive their
interest from the sentiments of piety and reverence for the modest virtues
and simple manners of human life with which they may be contemplated. A
man must be very insensible who would not be touched with pleasure at the
sight of the chapel of Buttermere, so strikingly expressing, by its diminutive
size, how small must be the congregation there assembled, as it were, like one
family; and proclaiming at the same time to the passenger, in connection with
the surrounding mountains, the depth of that seclusion in which the people
live, that has rendered necessary the building of a separate place of worship
for so few. A patriot, calling to mind the images of the stately fabrics
of Canterbury, York, or Westminster, will find a heart-felt satisfaction
in presence of this lowly pile, as a monument of the wise institutions of
our country, and as evidence of the all-pervading and paternal care of
that venerable Establishment, of which it is, perhaps, the humblest

Askham Church by William Green. A place of worship of a style not less
appropriate and admirable than that of the dwelling houses and other structures.
'How sacred the spirit by which our forefathers were directed! The *religio loci* is
no where violated by these unstinted yet unpretending works of human hands.'

daughter.   The edifice is scarcely larger than many of the single stones or
fragments of rock which are scattered near it.

We have thus far confined our observations on this division of the subject,
to that part of these Dales which runs up far into the mountains.

As we descend towards the open country, we meet with halls and
mansions, many of which have been places of defence against the incursions
of the Scottish borderers; and they not unfrequently retain their towers and
battlements.   To these houses, parks are sometimes attached, and to their
successive proprietors we chiefly owe whatever ornament is still left to the
country of majestic timber.   Through the open parts of the vales are
scattered, also, houses of a middle rank between the pastoral cottage and the
old hall residence of the knight or esquire.   Such houses differ much from
the rugged cottages before described, and are generally graced with a little
court or garden in front, where may yet be seen specimens of those fantastic
and quaint figures which our ancestors were fond of shaping out in yew-tree,
holly, or box-wood.   The passenger will sometimes smile at such elaborate
display of petty art, while the house does not deign to look upon the natural
beauty or the sublimity which its situation almost unavoidably commands.

Thus has been given a faithful description, the minuteness of which the
reader will pardon, of the face of this country as it was, and had been through
centuries, till within the last sixty years.   Towards the head of these Dales
was found a perfect Republic of Shepherds and Agriculturists, among whom
the plough of each man was confined to the maintenance of his own family, or

Kentmere Hall, near Kendal, wash drawing by John Harden, c. 1816. A house of 'a middle rank between the pastoral cottage and the old hall residence of the knight or squire.' Dwellings like this, with peel towers as a 'defence against the incursions of the Scottish borderers', are common on the fringes of the Lake District.

to the occasional accommodation of his neighbour.*   Two or three cows furnished each family with milk and cheese.   The chapel was the only edifice that presided over these dwellings, the supreme head of this pure Commonwealth; the members of which existed in the midst of a powerful empire, like an ideal society or an organized community, whose constitution had been imposed and regulated by the mountains which protected it.   Neither high-born nobleman, knight, nor esquire, was here; but many of these humble sons of the hills had a consciousness that the land, which they walked over and tilled, had for more than five hundred years been possessed by men of their name and blood; and venerable was the transition, when a curious traveller, descending from the heart of the mountains, had come to some ancient manorial residence in the more open parts of the Vales, which, through the rights attached to its proprietor, connected the almost visionary mountain republic he had been contemplating with the substantial frame of society as existing in the laws and constitution of a mighty empire.

* One of the most pleasing characteristics of manners in secluded and thinly-populated districts, is a sense of the degree in which human happiness and comfort are dependent on the contingency of neighbourhood.   This is implied by a rhyming adage common here, "*Friends are far, when neighbours are nar*" (near).   This mutual helpfulness is not confined to out-of-doors work; but is ready upon all occasions.   Formerly, if a person became sick, especially the mistress of a family, it was usual for those of the neighbours who were more particularly connected with the party by amicable offices, to visit the house, carrying a present; this practice, which is by no means obsolete, is called *owning* the family, and is regarded as a pledge of a disposition to be otherwise serviceable in a time of disability and distress.

SECTION THIRD

CHANGES, AND RULES OF TASTE
FOR PREVENTING THEIR BAD EFFECTS

SUCH, as hath been said, was the appearance of things till within the last sixty years. A practice, denominated Ornamental Gardening, was at that time becoming prevalent over England. In union with an admiration of this art, and in some instances in opposition to it, had been generated a relish for select parts of natural scenery: and Travellers, instead of confining their observations to Towns, Manufactories, or Mines, began (a thing till then unheard of) to wander over the island in search of sequestered spots, distinguished as they might accidentally have learned, for the sublimity or beauty of the forms of Nature there to be seen. Dr. Brown, the celebrated Author of the Estimate of the Manners and Principles of the Times, published a letter to a friend, in which the attractions of the Vale of Keswick were delineated with a powerful pencil, and the feeling of a genuine Enthusiast. Gray, the Poet, followed: he died soon after his forlorn and melancholy pilgrimage to the Vale of Keswick, and the record left behind him of what he had seen and felt in this journey, excited that pensive interest with which the human mind is ever disposed to listen to the farewell words of a man of genius. The journal of Gray feelingly showed how the gloom of ill health and low spirits had been irradiated by objects, which the Author's powers of mind enabled him to describe with distinctness and unaffected simplicity. Every reader of this journal must have been impressed with the words which conclude his notice of the Vale of Grasmere:—"Not a single red tile, no flaring gentleman's house or garden-wall, breaks in upon the repose of this little unsuspected paradise; but all is peace, rusticity, and happy povery, in its neatest and most becoming attire."

What is here so justly said of Grasmere applied almost equally to all its sister Vales. It was well for the undisturbed pleasure of the Poet that he had no forebodings of the change which was soon to take place; and it might have been hoped that these words, indicating how much the charm of what *was*, depended upon what was *not*, would of themselves have preserved the ancient franchises of this and other kindred mountain retirements from trespass; or (shall I dare to say?) would have secured scenes so consecrated from profanation. The lakes had now become celebrated; visitors flocked hither from all parts of England; the fancies of some were smitten so deeply, that they became settlers; and the Islands of Derwentwater and

Grasmere from Red Bank by L. Aspland. It was the view from Red Bank which
first delighted Wordsworth. This popular print, with the foreground arranged
in the conventional picturesque manner, was published in about 1850. It shows
'the solitary green island', beloved and frequently visited by the Wordsworths,
the rectory by the church where they lived for two years, and on the left Allan
Bank, the house which Wordsworth decried as an 'abomination', and then
occupied.

Belle Isle Lodge on the Great Island in Windermere in 1791, by John 'Warwick' Smith. The circular house, built in 1774 to the designs of John Plaw, 'the first house that was built in the Lake District for the sake of the beauty of the country [the first picturesque house], was the work of Mr English, who had travelled in Italy'. The house reflects the taste for placing buildings, reminiscent of those in the idyllic pictures of Claude Lorrain, in picturesque landscape gardens. Wordsworth lamented the 'setting up a length of garden-wall, as exclusive as it was ugly . . . the nuisance was swept away when the late Mr Curwen became owner of this favoured spot' (in 1781). The house is still occupied by the Curwen family.

Windermere and Belle Isle, pen and wash drawing
by E. Becker. The drawing is in the manner of Claude with the round house
placed like a temple in the middle distance, and the tree and the boat framing the
prospect in the foreground. Wordsworth frequently comments on the beauty of
the landscape seen from a boat on Windermere.

Winandermere, as they offered the strongest temptation, were the first places seized upon, and were instantly defaced by the intrusion.

The venerable wood that had grown for centuries round the small house called St. Herbert's Hermitage, had inded some years before been felled by its native proprietor, and the whole island planted anew with Scotch firs, left to spindle up by each other's side — a melancholy phalanx, defying the power of the winds, and disregarding the regret of the spectator, who might otherwise have cheated himself into a belief, that some of the decayed remains of those oaks, the place of which was in this manner usurped, had been planted by the Hermit's own hand: This sainted spot, however, suffered comparatively little injury. At the bidding of an alien improver, the Hind's Cottage, upon Vicar's island, in the same lake, with its embowering sycamores and cattle-shed, disappeared from the corner where they stood; and right in the middle, and upon the precise point of the island's highest elevation, rose a tall square habitation, with four sides exposed like an astronomer's observatory, or a warren-house reared upon an eminence for the detection of depredators, or, like the temple of Œolus, where all the winds pay him obeisance. Round this novel structure, but at a respectful distance, platoons of firs were stationed, as if to protect their commander when weather and time should somewhat have shattered his strength. Within the narrow limits of this island were typified also the state and strength of a kingdom, and its religion as it had been, and was,—for neither was the druidical circle uncreated, nor the church of the present establishment; nor the stately pier, emblem of commerce and navigation; nor the fort to deal out thunder upon the approaching invader. The taste of a succeeding proprietor rectified the mistakes as far as was practicable, and has ridded the spot of its puerilities. The church, after being docked of its steeple, is applied both ostensibly and really, to the purpose for which the body of the pile was actually erected, namely, a boat-house; the fort is demolished; and, without indignation on the part of the spirits of the ancient Druids who officiated at the circle upon the opposite hill, the mimic arrangement of stones, with its *sanctum sanctorum*, has been swept away.

The present instance has been singled out, extravagant as it is, because, unquestionably, this beautiful country has, in numerous other places, suffered from the same spirit, though not clothed exactly in the same form, nor active in an equal degree. It will be sufficient here to utter a regret for the changes that have been made upon the principal Island at Winandermere, and in its neighbourhood. What could be more unfortunate than the taste that suggested the paring of the shores, and surrounding with an embankment this spot of ground, the natural shape of which was so beautiful! An artificial appearance has thus been given to the whole, while infinite varieties of minute beauty have been destroyed. Could not the margin of this noble island be given back to nature? Winds and waves work with a careless and graceful hand: and, should they in some places carry away a portion of the soil, the trifling loss would be amply compensated by the additional spirit, dignity, and loveliness, which these agents and the other powers of nature would soon communicate to what was left behind. As to the larch-plantations upon the main shore,—they who remember the original appearance of the rocky steeps, scattered over with native hollies and ash-trees, will be prepared to agree with what I shall have to say hereafter upon plantations* in general.

But, in truth, no one can now travel through the more frequented tracts, without being offended, at almost every turn, by an introduction of discordant objects, disturbing that peaceful harmony of form and colour, which had been through a long lapse of ages most happily preserved.

All gross transgressions of this kind originate, doubtless, in a feeling natural and honourable to the human mind, viz, the pleasure which it receives from distinct ideas, and from the perception of order, regularity, and contrivance. Now, unpractised minds receive these impressions only from

* These are disappearing fast, under the management of the present Proprietor, and native wood is resuming its place.

A view of the middle part of Windermere as idealized by William Gilpin. This illustration in Gilpin's *Observations on the Mountains and Lakes* interprets the actual scene more accurately than most of his picturesque rearrangements of nature. The round house on Belle Isle is, for instance, discernible.

objects that are divided from each other by strong lines of demarcation; hence the delight with which such minds are smitten by formality and harsh contrast.   But I would beg of those who are eager to create the means of such gratification, first carefully to study what already exists; and they will find, in a country so lavishly gifted by nature, an abundant variety of forms marked out with a precision that will satisfy their desires.   Moreover, a new habit of pleasure will be formed opposite to this, arising out of the perception of the fine gradations by which in nature one thing passes away into another, and the boundaries that constitute individuality disappear in one instance only to be revived elsewhere under a more alluring form.   The hill of Dunmallet, at the foot of Ulswater, was once divided into different portions, by avenues of fir-trees, with a green and almost perpendicular lane descending down the steep hill through each avenue;—contrast this quaint appearance with the image of the same hill overgrown with self-planted wood,—each tree springing up in the situation best suited to its kind, and with that shape which the situation constrained or suffered it to take. What endless melting and playing into each other of forms and colours does the one offer to a mind at once attentive and active; and how insipid and lifeless, compared with it, appear those parts of the former exhibition with which a child, a peasant perhaps, or a citizen unfamiliar with natural imagery, would have been most delighted!

The disfigurement which this country has undergone, has not, however, proceeded wholly from the common feelings of human nature which have been referred to as the primary sources of bad taste in rural imagery; another cause must be added, that has chiefly shown itself in its effect upon buildings. I mean a warping of the natural mind occasioned by a consciousness that, this country being an object of general admiration, every new house would be looked at and commented upon either for approbation or censure. Hence all the deformity and ungracefulness that ever pursue the steps of constraint or affectation. Persons, who in Leicestershire or Northamptonshire would probably have built a modest dwelling like those of their sensible neighbours, have been turned out of their course; and, acting a part, no wonder if, having had little experience, they act it ill. The craving for prospect, also, which is immoderate, particularly in new settlers, has rendered it impossible that buildings, whatever might have been their architecture, should in most instances be ornamental to the landscape; rising as they do from the summits of naked hills in staring contrast to the snugness and privacy of the ancient houses.

No man is to be condemned for a desire to decorate his residence and possessions; feeling a disposition to applaud such an endeavour, I would show how the end may be best attained. The rule is simple; with respect to grounds—work, where you can, in the spirit of nature, with an invisible hand of art. Planting, and a removal of wood, may thus, and thus only, be carried on with good effect; and the like may be said of building, if Antiquity, who may be styled the co-partner and sister of Nature, be not denied the respect to which she is entitled. I have already spoken of the beautiful forms of the ancient mansions of this country, and of the happy manner in which they harmonise with the forms of nature. Why cannot such be taken as a model, and modern internal convenience be confined within their external grace and dignity. Expense to be avoided, or difficulties to be overcome, may prevent a close adherence to this model; still, however, it might be followed to a certain degree in the style of architecture and in the choice of situation, if the thirst for prospect were mitigated by those considerations of comfort, shelter, and convenience, which used to be chiefly sought after. But should an aversion to old fashions unfortunately exist, acompanied with a desire to transplant into the cold and stormy North, the elegancies of a villa formed upon a model taken from countries with a milder climate, I will adduce a passage from an English poet, the divine Spenser, which will show in what manner such a plan may be realised without injury to the native beauty of these scenes.

> Into that forest farre they thence him led,
> Where was their dwelling in a pleasant glade
> With MOUNTAINS round about environed,

And MIGHTY WOODS which did the valley shade,
And like a stately theatre it made,
Spreading itself into a spacious plaine;
And in the midst a little river plaide
Emongst the puny stones which seem'd to 'plaine
With gentle murmure that his course they did restraine.

Beside the same dainty place there lay,
Planted with mirtle trees and laurels green,
In which the birds sang many a lovely lay
Of God's high praise, and of their sweet loves teene,
As it an earthly paradise had beene;
In whose *enclosed shadow* there was pight
A fair pavillion, *scarcely to be seen*,
The which was all within most richly dight,
That greatest princes living it mote well delight.

Houses or mansions suited to a mountainous region, should be "not obvious, not obtrusive, but retired;" and the reasons for this rule, though they have been little adverted to, are evident. Mountainous countries, more frequently and forcibly than others, remind us of the power of the elements, as manifested in the winds, snows, and torrents, and accordingly make the notion of exposure very unpleasing; while shelter and comfort are in proportion necessary and acceptable. Far-winding vallies difficult of access, and the feelings of simplicity habitually connected with mountain retirements, prompt us to turn from ostentation as a thing there eminently unnatural and out of place. A mansion, amid such scenes, can never have sufficient dignity or interest to become principal in the landscape, and to render the mountains, lakes, or torrents, by which it may be surrounded, a subordinate part of the view. It is, I grant, easy to conceive, that an ancient castellated building, hanging over a precipice or raised upon an island, or the peninsula of a lake, like that of Kilchurn Castle, upon Loch Awe, may not want, whether deserted or inhabited, sufficient majesty to preside for a moment in the spectator's thoughts over the high mountains among which it is embosomed; but its titles are from antiquity—a power readily submitted to upon occasion as the vicegerent of Nature: it is respected, as having owed its existence to the necessities of things, as a monument of security in times of disturbance and danger long passed away,—as a record of the pomp and violence of passion, and a symbol of the wisdom of law;—it bears a countenance of authority, which is not impaired by decay.

Child of loud-throated war, the mountain-stream
Roars in thy hearing; but thy hour of rest
Is come, and thou art silent in thy age!

To such honours a modern edifice can lay no claim; and the puny efforts of elegance appear contemptible, when, in such situations, they are obtruded in rivalship with the sublimities of Nature. But, towards the verge of a district like this of which we are treating, where the mountains subside into hills of moderate elevation, or in an undulating or flat country, a gentleman's mansion may, with propriety, become a principal feature in the landscape;

119

and, itself being a work of art, works and traces of artificial ornament may, without censure, be extended around it, as they will be referred to the common centre, the house; the right of which to impress within certain limits a character of obvious ornament will not be denied, where no commanding forms of nature dispute it, or set it aside. Now, to a want of the perception of this difference, and to the causes before assigned, may chiefly be attributed the disfigurement which the Country of the Lakes has undergone, from persons who may have built, demolished, and planted, with full confidence, that every change and addition was or would become an improvement.

The principle that ought to determine the position, apparent size, and architecture of a house, viz. that it should be so constructed, and (if large) so much of it hidden, as to admit of its being gently incorporated into the scenery of nature—should also determine its colour. Sir Joshua Reynolds used to say, "If you would fix upon the best colour for your house, turn up a stone, or pluck up a handful of grass by the roots, and see what is the colour of the soil where the house is to stand, and let that be your choice." Of course, this precept given in conversation, could not have been meant to be taken literally. For example, in Low Furness, where the soil, from its strong impregnation with iron, is universally of a deep red, if this rule were strictly followed, the house also must be of a glaring red; in other places it must be of a sullen black; which would only be adding annoyance to annoyance. The rule, however, as a general guide, is good; and, in agricultural districts, where large tracts of soil are laid bare by the plough, particularly if (the face of the country being undulating) they are held up to view, this rule, though not to be implicitly adhered to, should never be lost sight of;—the colour of the house ought, if possible, to have a cast or shade of the colour of the soil. The principle is, that the house must harmonise with the surrounding landscape: accordingly, in mountainous countries, with still more confidence may it be said, "look at the rocks and those parts of the mountains where the soil is visible, and they will furnish a safe direction." Nevertheless, it will often happen that the rocks may bear so large a proportion to the rest of the landscape, and may be of such a tone of colour, that the rule may not admit, even here, of being implicitly followed. For instance, the chief defect in the colouring of the Country of the Lakes (which is most strongly felt in the summer season) is an over-prevalence of a bluish tint, which the green of the herbage, the fern, and the woods, does not sufficently counteract. If a house, therefore, should stand where this defect prevails, I have no hesitation in saying, that the colour of the neighbouring rocks would not be the best that could be chosen. A tint ought to be introduced approaching nearer to those which, in the technical language of painters, are called *warm* : this, if happily selected, would not disturb, but would animate the landscape. How often do we see this exemplified upon a small scale by the native cottages, in cases

Opposite: Rydal Water.

Honister Pass.

Windermere from Orrest Head, by James Baker Pyne. 'I overlooked the bed of Windermere Like a vast river, stretching in the sun.' This view from Orrest Head was particularly dear to Wordsworth, and it is ironical that in the last three years of his life it embraced the new Windermere railway station, with steam locomotives puffing in and out.

Bassenthwaite Lake at night, watercolour by James Bourne. 'A shining mirror to the moon's pale orb,/which, dim and waning, o'er the shadowy cliffs,/The solemn woods, and spiry mountain tops,/Her glimmering faintness threw.' Quoted by Wordsworth from John Brown's *Letter*.

Devoke Water by Blacklock, which lies high up on the southern side of Eskdale close to the track leading to Ulpha in the Duddon Valley, and only five miles from the sea. 'In the bosom of . . . Devockwater is a single rock, which, owing to its neighbourhood to the sea, is—"The haunt of cormorants and sea-mew's clang," a music well suited to the stern and wild character of the several scenes!'

where the glare of white-wash has been subdued by time and enriched by weather-stains! No harshness is then seen; but one of these cottages, thus coloured, will often form a central point to a landscape by which the whole shall be connected, and an influence of pleasure diffused over all the objects that compose the picture. But where the cold blue tint of the rocks is enriched by the iron tinge, the colour cannot be too closely imitated; and it will be produced of itself by the stones hewn from the adjoining quarry, and by the mortar, which may be tempered with the most gravelly part of the soil. The pure blue gravel, from the bed of the river, is, however, more suitable to the mason's purpose, who will probably insist also that the house must be covered with rough-cast, otherwise it cannot be kept dry; if this advice be taken, the builder of taste will set about contriving such means as may enable him to come the nearest to the effect aimed at.

The supposed necessity of rough-cast to keep out rain in houses not built of hewn stone or brick, has tended greatly to injure English landscape, and the neighbourhood of these Lakes especially, by furnishing such apt occasion for whitening buildings. That white should be a favorite colour for rural residences is natural for many reasons. The mere aspect of cleanliness and neatness thus given, not only to an individual house, but, where the practice is general, to the whole face of the country, produces moral associations so powerful, that, in many minds, they take place of all others. But what has already been said upon the subject of cottages, must have convinced men of feeling and imagination, that a human dwelling of the humblest class may be rendered more deeply interesting to the affections, and far more pleasing to the eye, by other influences, than a sprightly tone of colour spread over its outside. I do not, however, mean to deny, that a small white building, embowered in trees, may, in some situations, be a delightful and animating object—in no way injurious to the landscape; but this only where it sparkles from the midst of a thick shade, and in rare and solitary instances; especially if the country be itself rich and pleasing, and abound with grand forms. On the sides of bleak and desolate moors, we are indeed thankful for the sight of white cottages and white houses plentifully scattered, where, without these, perhaps everything would be cheerless: this is said, however, with hesitation, and with a wilful sacrifice of some higher enjoyments. But I have certainly seen such buildings glittering at sunrise, and in wandering lights, with no common pleasure. The continental traveller also will remember, that the convents hanging from the rocks of the Rhine, the Rhone, the Danube, or among the Appenines, or the mountains of Spain, are not looked at with less complacency when, as is often the case, they happen to be a brilliant white. But this is perhaps owing, in no small degree, to the contrast of that lively colour with the gloom of monastic life, and to the general want of rural residences of smiling and attractive appearance, in those countries.

The objections to white, as a colour, in large spots or masses in landscape, especially in a mountainous country, are insurmountable. In nature, pure white is scarcely ever found but in small objects, such as flowers; or in those which are transitory, as the clouds, foam of rivers, and snow. Mr. Gilpin, who notices this, has also recorded the just remark of Mr. Locke, of N——, that white destroys the *gradations* of distance; and, therefore, an object of pure white can scarcely ever be managed with good effect in landscape-painting. Five or six white houses, scattered over a valley, by their obtrusiveness, dot the surface, and divide it into triangles, or other mathematical figures, haunting the eye, and disturbing that repose which might otherwise be perfect. I have seen a single white house materially impair the majesty of a mountain; cutting away, by a harsh separation, the whole of its base below the point on which the house stood. Thus was the apparent size of the mountain reduced, not by the interposition of another object in a manner to call forth the imagination, which will give more than the eye loses; but what had been abstracted in this case was left visible; and the mountain appeared to take its beginning, or to rise, from the line of the house, instead of its own natural base. But, if I may express my own individual feeling, it is after sunset, at the coming on of twilight, that white objects are most to be complained of. The solemnity and quietness of nature at that time are always marred, and often destroyed by them. When the ground is covered with snow, they are of course inoffensive; and in moonshine they are always pleasing—it is a tone of light with which they accord: and the dimness of the scene is enlivened by an object at once conspicuous and cheerful. I will conclude this subject with noticing, that the cold, slaty colour, which many persons, who have heard the white condemned, have adopted in its stead, must be disapproved of for the reason already given. The flaring yellow runs into the opposite extreme, and is still more censurable. Upon the whole, the safest colour, for general use, is something between a cream and a dust-colour, commonly called stone colour;—there are, among the Lakes, examples of this that need not be pointed out.*

The principle taken as our guide, viz. that the house should be so formed, and of such apparent size and colour, as to admit of its being gently incorporated with the works of nature, should also be applied to the management of the grounds and plantations, and is here more urgently needed; for it is from abuses in this department, far more even than from the introduction of exotics in architecture (if the phrase may be used), that this country has suffered. Larch and fir plantations have been spread, not merely with a view to profit, but in many instances for the sake of ornament. To those who plant for profit, and are thrusting every other tree out of the way, to make room for their favourite, the larch, I would utter first a regret, that they should have selected these lovely vales for their vegetable manufactory, when there is so much barren and irreclaimable land in the neighbouring moors, and in other parts of the island, which might have been had for this purpose at a far cheaper rate. And I will also beg leave to represent to them, that they ought not to be carried away by flattering promises from the speedy growth of this tree; because in rich soils and sheltered situations, the wood, though it thrives fast, is full of sap, and of little value; and is, likewise, very subject to ravage from the attacks of insects, and

---

* A proper colouring of houses is now becoming general. It is best that the colouring material should be mixed with the rough-cast, and not laid on as a *wash* afterwards.

'Keswick', watercolour by Francis Wheatley. Don Manuel Alvarez Espriella in *Letters from England*, 1807, commented on the carts in the Lake District, with strange wheels like those in Wheatley's picture, the like of which he had only seen in his native Spain. The Spanish traveller was actually Robert Southey, writing under an assumed name.

from blight. Accordingly, in Scotland, where planting is much better understood, and carried on upon an incomparably larger scale than among us, good soil and sheltered situations are appropriated to the the oak, the ash, and other deciduous trees; and the larch is now generally confined to barren and exposed ground. There the plant, which is a hardy one, is of slower growth; much less liable to injury; and the timber is of better quality. But the circumstances of many permit, and their taste leads them, to plant with little regard to profit; and there are others, less wealthy, who have such a lively feeling of the native beauty of these scenes, that they are laudably not unwilling to make some sacrifices to heighten it. Both these classes of persons, I would entreat to enquire of themselves wherein that beauty which they admire consists. They would then see that, after the feeling has been gratified that prompts us to gather round our dwelling a few flowers and shrubs, which from the circumstance of their not being native, may, by their very looks, remind us that they owe their existence to our hands, and their prosperity to our care; they will see that, after this natural desire has been provided for, the course of all beyond has been predetermined by the spirit of the place. Before I proceed, I will remind those who are not satisfied with the restraint thus laid upon them, that they are liable to a charge of inconsistency, when they are so eager to change the face of that country, whose native attractions, by the act of erecting their habitations in it, they have so emphatically acknowledged. And surely there is not a single spot that would not have, if well managed, sufficient dignity to support itself, unaided by the productions of other climates, or by elaborate decorations which might be becoming elsewhere.

Having adverted to the feelings that justify the introduction of a few exotic plants, provided they be confined almost to the doors of the house, we may add, that a transition should be contrived, without abruptness, from these foreigners to the rest of the shrubs, which ought to be of the kinds scattered by Nature, through the woods—holly, broom, wild-rose, elder, dogberry, white and black thorn &c.—either these only, or such as are carefully selected in consequence of their being united in form, and harmonising in colour with them, especially with respect to colour, when the tints are most diversified, as in autumn and spring. The various sorts of fruit-and-blossom-bearing trees usually found in orchards, to which may be added those of the woods,—namely, the wilding, black cherry tree, and wild cluster-cherry (here called heck-berry)—may be happily admitted as an intermediate link between the shrubs and the forest trees; which last ought almost entirely to be such as are native of the country. Of the birch, one of the most beautiful of the native trees, it may be noticed, that, in dry and rocky situations, it outstrips even the larch, which many persons are tempted to plant merely on account of the speed of its growth. The Scotch fir is less attractive during its youth than any other plant; but, when full-grown, if it has had room to spread out its arms, it becomes a noble tree; and, by those who are disinterested enough to plant for posterity, it may be placed along with the sycamore near the house; for, from their massiveness, both these trees unite well with buildings, and in some situations with rocks also; having, in their forms and apparent substances, the effect of something intermediate betwixt the immoveableness and solidity of stone, and the spray and foliage of the lighter trees. If these general rules be just, what shall we say to whole acres of artificial shrubbery and exotic trees among rocks and dashing torrents, with their own wild wood in sight—where we have the whole contents of the nurseryman's catalogue jumbled together—colour at war with colour, and form with form?—among the most peaceful subjects of Nature's kingdom, everywhere discord, distraction, and bewilderment! But this deformity, bad as it is, is not so obtrusive as the small patches and large tracts of larch-plantations that are overrunning the hill sides. To justify our condemnation of these, let us again recur to Nature. The process, by which she forms woods and forests, is as follows. Seeds are scattered indiscriminately by winds, brought by waters, and dropped by birds. They perish, or produce, according as the soil and situation upon which they fall are suited to them: and under the same dependence, the seedling or the sucker, if not cropped by animals, (which Nature is often careful to prevent by fencing it about with brambles or other prickly shrubs) thrives, and the tree grows, sometimes single, taking its own shape without constraint, but for the most part compelled to conform itself to some law imposed upon it by its neighbours. From low and sheltered places, vegetation travels upwards to the more exposed; and the young plants are protected, and to a certain degree fashioned, by those that have preceeded them. The continuous mass of foliage which would be thus produced, is broken by rocks, or by glades or open places, where the browzing of animals has prevented the growth of wood. As vegetation ascends, the winds begin also to bear their part in moulding the forms of the trees; but, thus mutually protected, trees, though not of the hardiest kind, are enabled to climb high up the mountains. Gradually, however, by the quality of the ground, and by increasing exposure, a stop is put to their ascent; the hardy trees only are left: those also, by little and little, give way—and a wild and irregular boundary is established, graceful in its outline, and never contemplated without some feeling, more or less distinct, of the powers of Nature by which it is imposed.

Contrast the liberty that encourages, and the law that limits, this joint work of nature and time, with the disheartening necessities, restrictions, and disadvantages, under which the artificial planter must proceed, even he whom long observation and fine feeling have best qualified for his task. In the first place his trees, however well chosen and adapted to their several situations, must generally start all at the same time; and this necessity would of itself prevent that fine connection of parts, that sympathy and organization, if I may so express myself, which pervades the whole of a natural wood, and appears to the eye in its single trees, its masses of foliage, and their various colours, when they are held up to view on the side of a mountain; or when, spread over a valley, they are looked down upon from an eminence. It is therefore impossible, under any circumstances, for the artificial planter to rival the beauty of nature. But a moment's thought will show that, if ten thousand of this spiky tree, the larch, are stuck in at once upon the side of a hill, they can grow up into nothing but deformity; that, while they are suffered to stand, we shall look in vain for any of those appearances which are the chief sources of beauty in a natural wood.

It must be acknowledged that the larch, till it has outgrown the size of a shrub, shows, when looked at singly, some elegance in form and appearance, especially in spring, decorated, as it then is, by the pink tassels of its blossoms; but, as a tree, it is less than any other pleasing: its branches (for *boughs* it has none) have no variety in the youth of the tree, and little dignity, even when it attains its full growth; *leaves* it cannot be said to have, consequently neither affords shade nor shelter.   In spring the larch becomes green long before the native trees; and its green is so peculiar and vivid, that, finding nothing to harmonize with it, wherever it comes forth, a disagreeable speck is produced.   In summer, when all other trees are in their pride, it is of a dingy lifeless hue; in autumn of a spiritless unvaried yellow, and in winter it is still more lamentably distinguished from every other deciduous tree of the forest, for they seem only to sleep, but the larch appears absolutely dead.   If an attempt be made to mingle thickets, or a certain proportion of other forest-trees, with the larch, its horizontal branches intolerantly cut them down as with a scythe, or force them to spindle up to keep pace with it.   The terminating spike renders it impossible that the several trees, where planted in numbers, should ever blend together so as to form a mass or masses of wood.   Add thousands to tens of thousands, and the appearance is still the same—a collection of separate individual trees, obstinately presenting themselves as such; and which, from whatever point they are looked at, if but seen, may be counted upon the fingers.   Sunshine, or shadow, has little power to adorn the surface of such a wood; and the trees not carrying up their heads, the wind raises among them no majestic undulations.   It is indeed true, that, in countries where the larch is native, and where, without interruption, it may sweep from valley to valley, and from hill to hill, a sublime image may be produced by such a forest, in the same manner as by one composed of any other single tree, to the spreading of which no limits can be assigned.   For sublimity will never be wanting, where the sense of innumerable multitude is lost in, and alternates with, that of intense unity; and to the ready perception of this effect, similarity and almost identity of individual form and monotony of colour contribute.   But this feeling is confined to the native immeasurable forest; no artificial plantation can give it.

The foregoing observations will, I hope, (as nothing has been condemned or recommended without a substantial reason) have some influence upon those who plant for ornament merely.   To such as plant for profit, I have already spoken.   Let me then entreat that the native deciduous trees may be left in complete possession of the lower ground; and that plantations of larch, if introduced at all, may be confined to the highest and most barren tracts.   Interposition of rocks would there break the dreary uniformity of which we have been complaining; and the winds would take hold of the trees, and imprint upon their shapes a wildness congenial to their situation.

Having determined what kinds of trees must be wholly rejected, or at least very sparingly used, by those who are unwilling to disfigure the country; and having shown what kinds ought to be chosen; I should have given, if my limits had not already been overstepped, a few practical rules for the manner in which trees ought to be disposed in planting.   But to this subject I should attach little importance, if I could succeed in banishing such trees as introduce deformity, and could prevail upon the proprietor to confine himself, either to those found in the native woods, or to such as accord with them. This is, indeed, the main point; for, much as these scenes have been injured by what has been taken from them—buildings, trees, and woods, either through negligence, necessity, avarice, or caprice—it is not the removals, but the harsh *additions* that have been made, which are the worst grievance—a standing and unavoidable annoyance. Often have I felt this distinction, with mingled satisfaction and regret; for, if no positive deformity or discordance be substituted or super-induced, such is the benignity of Nature, that, take away from her beauty after beauty, and ornament after ornament, her appearance cannot be marred—the scars, if any be left, will gradually disappear before a healing spirit; and what remains will still be soothing and pleasing.

> Many hearts deplored
> The fate of those old trees; and oft with pain
> The traveller at this day will stop and gaze
> On wrongs which nature scarcely seems to heed:
> For sheltered places, bosoms, nooks, and bays,
> And the pure mountains, and the gentle Tweed,
> And the green silent pastures, yet remain.

There are few ancient woods left in this part of England upon which such indiscriminate ravage as is here "deplored," could now be committed. But, out of the numerous copses, fine woods might in time be raised, probably without sacrifice of profit, by leaving, at the periodical fellings, a due proportion of the healthiest trees to grow up into timber.—This plan has fortunately, in many instances, been adopted; and they, who have set the example, are entitled to the thanks of all persons of taste. As to the management of planting with reasonable attention to ornament, let the images of nature be your guide, and the whole secret lurks in a few words; thickets or underwoods—single trees—trees clustered or in groups—groves—unbroken woods, but with varied masses of foliage—glades—invisible or winding boundaries—in rocky districts, a seemly proportion of rock left wholly bare, and other parts half hidden—disagreeable objects concealed, and formal lines broken—trees climbing up to the horizon, and, in some places, ascending from its sharp edge, in which they are rooted, with the whole body of the tree appearing to stand in the clear sky—in other parts, woods surmounted by rocks utterly bare and naked, which add to the sense of height, as if vegetation could not thither be carried, and impress a feeling of duration, power of resistance, and security from change!

The author has been induced to speak thus at length, by a wish to preserve the native beauty of this delightful district, because still further changes in its appearance must inevitably follow, from the change of inhabitants and owners which is rapidly taking place.—About the same time that strangers began to be attracted to the country, and to feel a desire to settle in it, the difficulty, that would have stood in the way of their procuring situations, was lessened by an unfortunate alteration in the circumstances of the native peasantry, proceeding from a cause which then began to operate, and is now

The Derwent river and Borrowdale, by J. B. Pyne.
An unusual view of the Derwent pouring into the gorge which divides upper
Borrowdale from Derwentwater. Pyne shows the Bowder Stone as a tourist
attraction, and tourists encamped by the river. Artists during Wordsworth's
lifetime rarely portrayed snow-covered hills, like Glaramara in this picture.

felt in every house.   The family of each man, whether *estatesman* or farmer, formerly had a twofold support; first, the produce of his lands and flocks; and, secondly, the profit drawn from the employment of the women and children, as manufacturers; spinning their own wool in their own houses (work chiefly done in the winter season), and carrying it to market for sale.   Hence, however numerous the children, the income of the family kept pace with its increase.   But, by the invention and universal application of machinery, this second resource has been cut off; the gains being so far reduced, as not to be sought after but by a few aged persons disabled from other employment.   Doubtless, the invention of machinery has not been to these people a pure loss; for the profits arising from home-manufactures operated as a strong temptation to choose that mode of labour in neglect of husbandry.   They also participate in the general benefit which the island has derived from the increased value of the produce of land, brought about by the establishment of manufactories, and in the consequent quickening of agricultural industry.   But this is far from making them amends; and now that home-manufactures are nearly done away, though the women and children might, at many seasons of the year, employ themselves with advantage in the fields beyond what they are accustomed to do, yet still all possible exertion in this way cannot be rationally expected from persons whose agricultural knowledge is so confined, and, above all, where there must necessarily be so small a capital.   The consequence, then, is—that proprietors and farmers being no longer able to maintain themselves upon small farms, several are united in one, and the buildings go to decay, or are destroyed; and that the lands of the *estatesmen* being mortgaged, and the owners constrained to part with them, they fall into the hands of wealthy purchasers, who in like manner unite and consolidate; and, if they wish to become residents, erect new mansions out of the ruins of the ancient cottages, whose little enclosures, with all the wild graces that grew out of them, disappear.   The feudal tenure under which the estates are held has indeed done something towards checking this influx of new settlers; but so strong is the inclination, that these galling restraints are endured; and it is probable, that in a few years the country on the margin of the Lakes will fall almost entirely into the possession of gentry, either strangers or natives.   It is then much to be wished, that a better taste should prevail among these new proprietors; and, as they cannot be expected to leave things to themselves, that skill and knowledge should prevent unnecessary deviations from that path of simplicity and beauty along which, without design and unconciously, their humble predecessors have moved.   In this wish the author will be joined by persons of pure taste throughout the whole island, who, by their visits (often repeated) to the Lakes in the North of England, testify that they deem the district a sort of national property, in which every man has a right and interest who has an eye to perceive and a heart to enjoy.

MISCELLANEOUS
OBSERVATIONS

MR. WEST, in his well-known Guide to the Lakes, recommends, as the best season for visiting this country, the interval from the beginning of June to the end of August; and, the two latter months being a time of vacation and leisure, it is almost exclusively in these that strangers resort hither. But that season is by no means the best; the colouring of the mountains and woods, unless where they are diversified by rocks, is of too unvaried a green; and, as a large portion of the vallies is allotted to hay-grass, some want of variety is found there also. The meadows, however, are sufficiently enlivened after hay-making begins, which is much later than in the southern part of the island. A stronger objection is rainy weather, setting in sometimes at this period with a vigour, and continuing with a perseverance, that may remind the disappointed and dejected traveller of those deluges of rain which fall among the Abyssinian mountains, for the annual supply of the Nile. The months of September and October (particularly October) are generally attended with much finer weather; and the scenery is then, beyond comparison, more diversified, more splendid, and beautiful; but, on the other hand, short days prevent long excursions, and sharp and chill gales are unfavourable to parties of pleasure out of doors. Nevertheless, to the sincere admirer of nature, who is in good health and spirits, and at liberty to make a choice, the six weeks following the 1st of September may be recommended in preference to July and August. For there is no inconvenience arising from the season which, to such a person, would not be amply compensated by the *autumnal* appearance of any of the more retired vallies, into which discordant plantations and unsuitable buildings have not yet found entrance. — In such spots, at this season, there is an admirable compass and proportion of natural harmony in colour, through the whole scale of objects; in the tender green of the after-grass upon the meadows, interspersed with islands of grey or mossy rock, crowned by shrubs and trees; in the irregular inclosures of standing corn, or stubble-fields, in like manner broken; in the mountain-sides glowing with fern of divers colours; in the calm blue lakes and river-pools; and in the foliage of the trees, through all the tints of autumn, — from the pale and brilliant yellow of the birch and ash, to the deep greens of the unfaded oak and alder, and of the ivy upon the rocks, upon the trees, and the cottages. Yet, as most travellers are either stinted, or

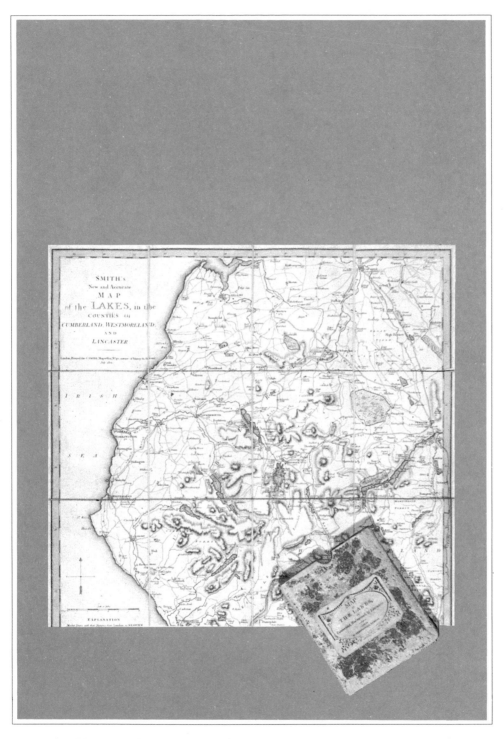

Smith's Map of the Lakes. First published in 1800, this was the earliest map of the Lake District intended to be carried by tourists. It was sold mounted on linen and folded in a slip case for the pocket.

stint themselves, for time, the space between the middle or last week in May, and the middle or last week of June, may be pointed out as affording the best combination of long days, fine weather, and variety of impressions.   Few of the native trees are then in full leaf; but, for whatever may be wanting in depth of shade, more than an equivalent will be found in the diversity of foliage, in the blossoms of the fruit-and-berry-bearing trees which abound in the woods, and in the golden flowers of the broom and other shrubs, with which many of the copses are interveined.   In those woods, also, and on these mountain-sides which have a northern aspect, and in the deep dells, many of the spring-flowers still linger; while the open and sunny places are stocked with the flowers of the approaching summer.   And, besides, is not an exquisite pleasure still untasted by him who has not heard the choir of linnets and thrushes chaunting their love-songs in the copses, woods, and hedge-rows of a mountainous country; safe from the birds of prey, which build in the inaccessible crags, and are at all hours seen or heard wheeling about in the air?   The number of these formidable creatures is probably the cause, why, in the *narrow* vallies, there are no skylarks; as the destroyer would be enabled to dart upon them from the near and surrounding crags,

136

Two pencil and chalk drawings by Edward Lear on his sketching tour in 1836.
Above: This view looking down Loweswater demonstrates that with
Derwentwater it is an exception to the precept that lakes appear to most
advantage when approached from their outlet, 'for by this way of approach, the
traveller faces the grander features of the scene'. *Opposite*: The familiar view
looking up Ullswater from Gowbarrow Park—'the majestic Lake, forced to take
a winding course by bold promontories, and environed by mountains of sublime
form, towering above each other.'

Windermere, looking south down the lake, watercolour by Francis Towne. This
view of the pellucid waters of the lower lake illustrates the clarity of the
reflections, often remarked on by Wordsworth, and his precept that views
towards the foot of a lake will normally be less dramatic than those
towards its head.

before they could descend to their ground-nests for protection. It is not
often that the nightingale resorts to these vales; but almost all the other tribes
of our English warblers are numerous; and their notes, when listened to by
the side of broad still waters, or when heard in unison with the murmuring of
mountain-brooks, have the compass of their power enlarged
accordingly. There is also an imaginative influence in the voice of the
cuckoo, when that voice has taken possession of a deep mountain valley, very
different from any thing which can be excited by the same sound in a flat
country. Nor must a circumstance be omitted, which here renders the close
of spring especially interesting; I mean the practice of bringing down the
ewes from the mountains to yean in the vallies and enclosed grounds. The
herbage being thus cropped as it springs, *that* first tender emerald green of
the season, which would otherwise have lasted little more than a fortnight, is
prolonged in the pastures and meadows for many weeks: while they are
farther enlivened by the multitude of lambs bleating and skipping
about. These sportive creatures, as they gather strength, are turned out
upon the open mountains, and with their slender limbs, their snow-white
colour, and their wild and light motions, beautifully accord or contrast with
the rocks and lawns, upon which they must now begin to seek their
food. And last, but not least, at this time the traveller will be sure of room
and comfortable accommodation, even in the smaller inns. I am aware that
few of those who may be inclined to profit by this recommendation will be
able to do so, as the time and manner of an excursion of this kind are mostly
regulated by circumstances which prevent an entire freedom of choice. It
will therefore be more pleasant to observe, that, though the months of July
and August are liable to many objections, yet it often happens that the
weather, at this time, is not more wet and stormy than they, who are really

capable of enjoying the sublime forms of nature in their utmost sublimity, would desire. For no traveller, provided he be in good health, and with any command of time, would have a just privilege to visit such scenes, if he could grudge the price of a little confinement among them, or interruption in his journey, for the sight or sound of a storm coming on or clearing away. Insensible must he be who would not congratulate himself upon the bold bursts of sunshine, the descending vapours, wandering lights and shadows, and the invigorated torrents and water-falls, with which broken weather, in a mountainous region, is accompanied. At such a time there is no cause to complain, either of the monotony of midsummer colouring, or the glaring atmosphere of long, cloudless, and hot days.

Thus far concerning the respective advantages and disadvantages of the different seasons for visiting this country. As to the order in which objects are best seen—a lake being composed of water flowing from higher grounds, and expanding itself till its receptacle is filled to the brim,—it follows that it will appear to most advantage when approached from its outlet, especially if the lake be in a mountainous country; for, by this way of approach, the traveller faces the grander features of the scene, and is gradually conducted into its most sublime recesses. Now, every one knows, that from amenity and beauty the transition to sublimity is easy and favourable; but the reverse is not so; for, after the faculties have been elevated, they are indisposed to humbler excitement.*

It is not likely that a mountain will be ascended without disappointment, if a wide range of prospect be the object, unless either the summit be reached before sun-rise, or the visitant remain there until the time of sun-set, and afterwards. The precipitous sides of the mountain, and the neighbouring summits, may be seen with effect under any atmosphere which allows them to be seen at all; but *he* is the most fortunate adventurer, who chances to be involved in vapours which open and let in an extent of country partially, or, dispersing suddenly, reveal the whole region from centre to circumference.

A stranger to a mountainous country may not be aware that his walk in the early morning ought to be taken on the eastern side of the vale, otherwise he will lose the morning light, first touching the tops and thence creeping down the sides of the opposite hills, as the sun ascends, or he may go to some central eminence, commanding both the shadows from the eastern , and the lights upon the western mountains. But, if the horizon line in the east be low, the western side may be taken for the sake of the reflections, upon the water, of light from the rising sun. In the evening, for like reasons, the contrary course should be taken.

---

* The only instances to which the foregoing observations do not apply, are Derwent-water and Lowes-water. Derwent is distinguished from all the other Lakes by being *surrounded* with sublimity: the fantastic mountains of Borrowdale to the south, the solitary majesty of Skiddaw to the north, the bold steeps of Wallow-crag and Lodore to the east, and to the west the clustering mountains of New-lands. Lowes-water is tame at the head, but towards its outlet has a magnificent assemblage of mountains. Yet as far as respects the formation of such receptacles, the general observation holds good: neither Derwent nor Lowes-water derive any supplies from the streams of those mountains that dignify the landscape towards the outlets.

The Jaws of Borrowdale by John 'Warwick' Smith,
the defile which separates the alluvial valley
of upper Borrowdale from Derwentwater.

Haweswater, watercolour by Edward Dayes, *c*. 1795. Wordsworth found Haweswater 'undefiled by the intrusion of bad taste', but today it is a reservoir.

Wray Castle, Windermere, by T. L. Aspland, built as a private house in 1840–47 by a Liverpool surgeon, Dr James Dawson, to the designs of H. P. Horner. Wordsworth said it 'added a dignified feature to the interesting scenery in the midst of which it stands'.

Ullswater, watercolour by William Turner of Oxford. 'A tall fir, through which the wind sings when the other trees are leafless.' The Scotch fir was accepted by Wordsworth, together with the sycamore, as the favourite of the cottagers chosen to screen their cottages.

Rydal Water.

Deepdale, by T. H. Fielding, 'the character of which Valley may be conjectured from its name. It is terminated by a cove, a cragg and gloomy abyss, with precipitous sides.'

Farmstead near Ambleside, watercolour by Ramsay Richad Reinagle, 1807 & 1808. 'Sir Joshua Reynolds used to say, "if you would fix upon the best colour for your house, turn up a stone or pluck up a handful of grass by the roots, and see what is the colour of the soil, where the house is to stand, and let that be your choice".'

Borrowdale, watercolour by Joshua Christal. 'The fantastic mountains of Borrowdale.'

After all, it is upon the *mind* which a traveller brings along with him that his acquisitions, whether of pleasure or profit, must principally depend.— May I be allowed a few words on this subject?

Nothing is more injurious to genuine feeling than the practice of hastily and ungraciously depreciating the face of one country by comparing it with that of another.   True it is Qui *bene* distinguit bene *docet*; yet fastidiousness is a wretched travelling companion; and the best guide to which, in matters of taste we can entrust ourselves, is a disposition to be pleased.   For example, if a traveller be among the Alps, let him surrender up his mind to the fury of the gigantic torrents, and take delight in the contemplation of their almost irresistible violence, without complaining of the monotony of their foaming course, or being disgusted with the muddiness of the water—apparent even where it is violently agitated.   In Cumberland and Westmorland, let not the comparative weakness of the streams prevent him from sympathising with such impetuosity as they possess; and, making the most of the present objects, let him, as he justly may do, observe with admiration the unrivalled brilliancy of the water, and that variety of motion, mood, and character, that arises out of the want of those resources by which the power of the streams in the Alps is supported.—Again, with respect to the mountains; though these are comparatively of diminutive size, though there is little of perpetual snow, and no voice of summer-avalanches is heard among them; and though traces left by the ravage of the elements are here comparatively rare and unimpressive, yet out of this very deficiency proceeds a sense of stability and permanence that is, to many minds, more grateful—

> While the course rushes to the sweeping breeze
> Sigh forth their ancient melodies.

Among the Alps are few places that do not preclude this feeling of tranquil sublimity.   Havoc, and ruin, and desolation, and encroachment, are everywhere more or less obtruded; and it is difficult, notwithstanding the naked loftiness of the *pikes*, and the snow-capped summits of the *mounts*, to escape from the depressing sensation, that the whole are in a rapid process of dissolution; and, were it not that the destructive agency must abate as the heights diminish, would, in time to come, be levelled with the plains.   Nevertheless, I would relish to the utmost the demonstrations of every species of power at work to effect such changes.

From these general views let us descend a moment to detail.   A stranger to mountain imagery naturally on his first arrival looks out for sublimity in every object that admits of it; and is almost always disappointed.   For this disappointment there exists, I believe, no general preventive; nor is it desirable that there should.   But with regard to one class of objects, there is a point in which injurious expectations may be easily corrected.   It is generally supposed that waterfalls are scarcely worth being looked at except after much rain, and that, the more swoln the stream, the more fortunate the spectator; but this however is true only of large cataracts with sublime accompaniments; and not even of these without some drawbacks.   In other instances, what becomes, at such a time, of that sense of refreshing coolness which can only be felt in dry and sunny weather, when the rocks, herbs, and flowers glisten with moisture diffused by the breath of the precipitous water? But, considering these things as objects of sight only, it may be observed that the principal charm of the smaller waterfalls or cascades consists in certain proportions of form and affinities of colour, among the component parts of the scene; and in the contrast maintained between the falling water and that which is apparently at rest, or rather settling gradually into quiet in the pool below. The beauty of such a scene, where there is naturally so much agitation, is also heightened, in a peculiar manner, by the *glimmering*, and, towards the verge of the pool, by the *steady*, reflection of the surrounding images. Now, all those delicate distinctions are destroyed by heavy floods, and the whole stream rushes along in foam and tumultuous confusion. A happy proportion of component parts is indeed noticeable among the landscapes of the North of England; and, in this characteristic essential to a perfect picture, they surpass the scenes of Scotland, and, in a still greater degree, those of Switzerland.

As a resident among the Lakes, I frequently hear the scenery of the country compared with that of the Alps; and therefore a few words shall be added to what has been incidentally said upon that subject.

If we could recall, to this region of lakes, the native pine-forests, with which many hundred years ago a large portion of the heights was covered, then, during spring and autumn, it might frequently, with much propriety, be compared to Switzerland,—the elements of the landscape would be the same—one country representing the other in miniature. Towns, villages, churches, rural seats, bridges and roads: green meadows and arable grounds, with their various produce, and deciduous woods of diversified foliage which occupy the vales and lower regions of the mountains, would, as in Switzerland, be divided by dark forests from ridges and round-topped heights covered with snow, and from pikes and sharp declivities imperfectly arrayed in the same glittering mantle: and the resemblance would be still more perfect on those days when vapours, resting upon, and floating around the summits, leave the elevation of the mountains less dependent upon the eye than on the imagination. But the pine-forests have wholly disappeared; and only during late spring and early autumn is realized here that assemblage of the imagery of different seasons, which is exhibited through the whole summer among the Alps,—winter in the distance,—and warmth, leafy woods, verdure and fertility at hand, and widely diffused.

Striking, then, from among the permanent materials of the landscape, that stage of vegetation which is occupied by pine-forests, and, above that, the perennial snows, we have mountains, the highest of which little exceed 3000 feet, while some of the Alps do not fall short of 14,000 or 15,000, and 8,000 or 10,000 is not an uncommon elevation. Our tracts of wood and water are almost as diminutive in comparison; therefore, as far as sublimity is dependent upon absolute bulk and height, and atmospherical influences in connection with these, it is obvious, that there can be no rival-ship. But a short residence among the British Mountains will furnish abundant proof, that, after a certain point of elevation, viz. that which allows of compact and fleecy clouds settling upon, or sweeping over, the summits, the sense of sublimity depends more upon form and relation of objects to each other than upon their actual magnitude; and, that an elevation of 3000 feet is sufficient to call forth in a most impressive degree the creative, and magnifying, and softening powers of the atmosphere.   Hence, on the score even of sublimity, the superiority of the Alps is by no means so great as might hastily be inferred;—and, as to the *beauty* of the lower regions of the Swiss Mountains, it is noticeable—that, as they are all regularly mown, their surface has nothing of that mellow tone and variety of hues by which mountain turf, that is never touched by the scythe, is distinguished.   On the smooth and steep slopes of the Swiss hills, these plots of verdure do indeed agreeably unite their colour with that of the deciduous trees, or make a lively contrast with the dark green pine-groves that define them, and among which they run in endless variety of shapes—but this is most pleasing *at first sight;* the permanent gratification of the eye requires finer gradations of tone, and a more delicate blending of hues into each other.   Besides, it is only in spring and late autumn that cattle animate by their presence the Swiss lawns; and, though the pastures of the higher regions where they feed during the summer are left in their natural state of flowery herbage, those pastures are so remote, that their texture and colour are of no consequence in the composition of any picture in which a lake of the Vales is a feature.   Yet in those lofty regions, how vegetation is invigorated by the genial climate of that country!   Among the luxuriant flowers there met with, groves, or forests, if I may so call them, of Monks-hood are frequently seen; the plant of deep, rich blue, and as tall as in our gardens; and this at an elevation where, in Cumberland, Icelandic moss would only be found, or the stony summits be utterly bare.

We have, then, for the colouring of Switzerland, *principally* a vivid green herbage, black woods, and dazzling snows, presented in masses with a grandeur to which no one can be insensible; but not often graduated by Nature into soothing harmony, and so ill suited to the pencil, that though abundance of good subjects may be there found, they are not such as can be deemed *characteristic* of the country; nor is this unfitness confined to colour; the forms of the mountains, though many of them in some points of view the noblest that can be conceived, are apt to run into spikes and needles, and present a jagged outline which has a mean effect, transferred to canvass.   This must have been felt by the ancient masters; for, if I am not mistaken, they have not left a single landscape, the materials of which are taken from the *peculiar* features of the Alps; yet Titian passed his life almost in their neighbourhood; the Poussins and Claude must have been well acquainted with their aspects; and several admirable painters, as Tibaldi and Luino, were born among the Italian Alps.   A few experiments have lately been made by Englishmen, but they only prove that courage, skill, and judgement, may surmount any obstacles; and it may be safely affirmed, that they who have done best in this bold adventure, will be the least likely to repeat the attempt.   But, though our scenes are better suited to painting than those of the Alps, I should be sorry to contemplate either country in reference to that art, further than as its fitness or unfitness for the pencil renders it more or less pleasing to the eye of the spectator, who has learned to observe and feel, chiefly from Nature herself.

Correct and incorrect mountains. A plate from Gilpin's *Observations* demonstrating that Saddleback forms 'disagreeable lines' and that 'many of the pointed summits of the Alps are objects rather of singularity than of beauty. Only the easy line pleases.' Wordsworth agreed that the Alps 'are apt to run to spikes and needles and present a jagged outline which has a mean effect . . .'

Deeming the points in which Alpine imagery is superior to British too obvious to be insisted upon, I will observe that the deciduous woods, though in many places unapproachable by the axe, and triumphing in the pomp and prodigality of Nature, have, in general,* neither the variety nor beauty which would exist in those of the mountains of Britain, if left to themselves. Magnificent walnut trees grow upon the plains of Switzerland; and fine trees, of that species, are found scattered over the hill-sides: birches also grow here and there in luxuriant beauty; but neither these, nor oaks, are ever a prevailing tree, nor can even be said to be common; and the oaks, as far as I had an opportunity of observing, are greatly inferior to those of Britain. Among the interior vallies the proportion of beeches and pines is so great that other trees are scarcely noticeable; and surely such woods are at all seasons much less agreeable than that rich and harmonious distribution of oak, ash, elm, birch, and alder, that formerly clothed the sides of Snowdon and Helvellyn; and of which no mean remains still survive at the head of Ulswater. On the Italian side of the Alps, chestnut and walnut-trees grow at a considerable height on the mountains; but, even there, the foliage is not equal in beauty to the "natural product" of this climate. In fact the sunshine of the South of Europe, so envied when heard of at a distance, is in many respects injurious to rural beauty, particularly as it incites to the cultivation of spots of ground which in colder climates would be left in the hands of nature, favouring at the same time the culture of plants that are more valuable on account of the fruit they produce to gratify the palate, than for affording pleasure to the eye, as materials of landscape. Take, for instance, the Promontory of Bellagio, so fortunate in its command of the three branches of the Lake of Como, yet the ridge of the Promontory itself, being for the most part covered with vines interspersed with olive trees, accords but ill with the vastness of the green unappropriated mountains, and derogates not a little from the sublimity of those finely contrasted pictures to which it is a fore-ground. The vine, when cultivated upon a large scale, notwithstanding all that may be said of it in poetry,† makes but a dull formal appearance in landscape; and the olive-tree (though one is loth to say so) is not more grateful to the eye than our common willow, which it much resembles; but the hoariness of hue, common to both, has in the aquatic plant an appropriate delicacy, harmonising with the situation in which it most delights. The same may no doubt be said of the olive among the dry rocks of Attica, but I

---

* The greatest variety of trees is found in the Valais.

† Lucretius has charmingly described a scene of this kind.
> Inque dies magis in montem succedere sylvas
> Cogebant, infráque locum concedere cultis:
> Prata, lacus, rivos, segetes, vinetaque læta
> Collibus et campis ut haberent, atque olearum
> *Crula* distinguens inter *plaga* currere posset
> Per tumulos, et convalleis, campósque profusa:
> Ut nunc esse vides vario distìncta lepore
> Omnia, quæ pomis intersita dulcibus ornant,
> Arbustisque tenent felicibus obsita circúm.

am speaking of it as found in gardens and vineyards in the North of Italy. At Bellagio, what Englishman can resist the temptation of substituting, in his fancy, for these formal treasures of cultivation, the natural variety of one of our parks—its pastured lawns, coverts of hawthorn, of wild-rose, and honeysuckle, and the majesty of forest trees?—such wild graces as the banks of Derwent-water shewed in the time of the Ratcliffes; and Gowbarrow Park, Lowther, and Rydal do at this day.

As my object is to reconcile a Briton to the scenery of his own country, though not at the expense of truth, I am not afraid of asserting that in many points of view our LAKES, also, are much more interesting that those of the Alps; first, as is implied above, from being more happily proportioned to the other features of the landscape; and next, both as being infinitely more pellucid, and less subject to agitation from the winds.* Como, (which may perhaps be styled the King of Lakes, as Lugano is certainly the Queen) is disturbed by a periodical wind blowing *from* the head in the morning, and *towards* it in the afternoon. The magnificent Lake of the four Cantons, especially its noblest division, called the Lake of Uri, is not only much agitated by winds, but in the night time is disturbed from the bottom, as I was told, and indeed as I witnessed, without any apparent commotion in the air; and when at rest, the water is not pure to the eye, but of a heavy green hue—as is that of all the other lakes, apparently according to the degree in which they are fed by melted snows. If the Lake of Geneva furnish an exception, this is probably owing to its vast extent, which allows the water to deposit its impurities. The water of the English lakes, on the contrary, being of a crystalline clearness, the reflections of the surrounding hills are frequently so lively, that it is scarcely possible to distinguish the point where the real object terminates, and its unsubstantial duplicate begins. The lower part of the Lake of Geneva, from its narrowness, must be much less subject to agitation than the higher divisions and, as the water is clearer than that of the other Swiss Lakes, it will frequently exhibit this appearance, though it is scarcely possible in an equal degree. During two comprehensive tours among the Alps, I did not observe, except on one of the smaller lakes, between Lugano and Ponte Tresa, a single instance of those beautiful repetitions of surrounding objects on the bosom of the water, which are so frequently seen here: not to speak of the fine dazzling trembling network, breezy motions, and streaks and circles of intermingled smooth and rippled water, which makes the surface of our lakes a field of endless variety. But among the

---

* It is remarkable that Como (as is probably the case with other Italian Lakes) is more troubled by storms in summer than in winter. Hence the propriety of the following verses.

> Lari! margine ubique confragoso
> Nulli cœlicolum negas sacellum
> Picto pariete saxeoque tecto;
> Hinc miracula multa navitarum
> Audis, nec placido refellis ore,
> Sed nova usque paras, Noto vel Euro
> *Æstivas* quatientibus cavernas,
> Vel surgentis ab Adduæ cubili
> Cæco grandinis imbre provoluto.   LANDOR

Ullswater and Lyulph's Tower by Joseph Farington.
Wordsworth and Coleridge both record how, on their walking tour in
November 1799, they saw 'deep within the bosom of the Lake, a magnificent
Castle, with towers and battlements' (Wordsworth); as 'the fog begins to clear
off from the Lake . . . & clings viscously to the Hill—all the objects on the
opposite Coast are hidden, and all those hidden are reflected in the Lake, Trees,
& the Castle [Lyulph's Tower] & the huge Crag that dwarfs it! Divine! . . .
Lyulph's Tower gleams like a Ghost, dim and shadowy.' A moment later 'the
Tower itself rises emerging out of the mist, two thirds wholly hidden, the
turrets quite clear—and a moment all is snatched away—Realities &
Shadows—(*The Note Books of Samuel Taylor Coleridge*, ed. Kathleen Coburn,
New York, 1957, vol. i, p. 553.)

Alps, where every thing tends to the grand and the sublime, in surfaces as well as in forms, if the lakes do not court the placid reflections of land objects those of first-rate magnitude make compensation, in some degree, by exhibiting those ever-changing fields of green, blue, and purple shadows or lights, (one scarcely knows which to name them) that call to mind a sea-prospect contemplated from a lofty cliff.

The subject of torrents and water-falls has already been touched upon; but it may be added that in Switzerland, the perpetual accompaniment of snow upon the higher regions takes much from the effect of foaming white streams; while, from their frequency, they obstruct each other's influence upon the mind of the spectator; and, in all cases, the effect of an individual cataract, excepting the great Fall of the Rhine at Schaffhausen, is diminished by the general fury of the stream of which it is a part.

Recurring to the reflections from still water, I will describe a singular phenomenon of this kind of which I was an eye-witness.

Walking by the side of Ulswater upon a calm September morning, I saw, deep within the bosom of the lake, a magnificent Castle, with towers and battlements, nothing could be more distinct than the whole edifice;—after gazing with delight upon it for some time, as upon a work of enchantment, I could not but regret that my previous knowledge of the place enabled me to account for the appearance.   It was in fact the reflection of a pleasure-house called Lyulph's Tower—the towers and battlements magnified and so much changed in shape as not to be immediately recognized.   In the meanwhile, the pleasure-house itself was altogether hidden from my view by a body of vapour stretching over it and along the hill-side on which it stands, but not so as to have intercepted its communication with the lake; and hence this novel and most impressive object, which, if I had been a stranger to the spot, would, from its being inexplicable, have long detained the mind in a state of pleasing astonishment.

Appearances of this kind, acting upon the credulity of early ages, may have given birth to, and favoured the belief in, stories of subaqueous palaces, gardens, and pleasure-grounds—the brilliant ornaments of Romance.

With this *inverted* scene I will couple a much more extraordinary phenomenon, which will shew how other elegant fancies may have had their origin, less in invention than in the actual processes of nature.

About eleven o'clock on the forenoon of a winter's day, coming suddenly, in company of a friend, into view of the Lake of Grasmere, we were alarmed by the sight of a newly-created Island; the transitory thought of the moment was, that it had been produced by an earthquake or some other convulsion of nature.   Recovering from the alarm, which was greater than the reader can possibly sympathize with, but which was shared to its full extent by my companion, we proceeded to examine the object before us.   The elevation of this new island exceeded considerably that of the old one, its neighbour; it was likewise larger in circumference, comprehending a space of about five acres; its surface rocky, speckled with snow, and sprinkled over with birch trees; it was divided towards the south from the other island by a narrow frith, and in like manner from the northern shore of the lake; on the east and west it was separated from the shore by a much larger space of smooth water.

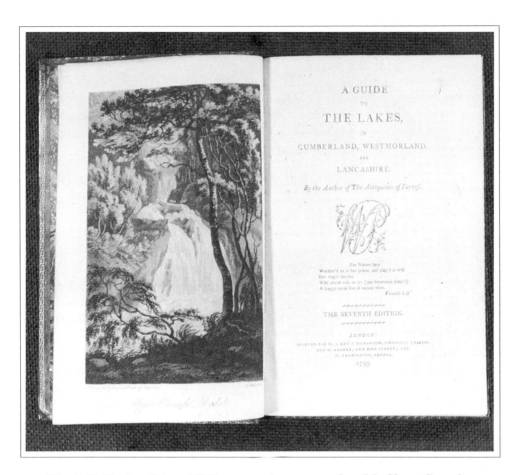

West's *Guide*, the edition of 1799, open to show an aquatint of the Upper Cascade, Rydal, engraved by S. Alken from a drawing by J. Emes after a sketch by Laporte. West's *Guide*, originally published in 1778 and republished posthumously in 1780, extensively revised and augmented by William Cockin, was still the standard guide fifty years later when Wordsworth's *Guide* began to come into general use. The eleventh and final edition was published in 1821.

Marvellous was the illusion! Comparing the new with the old Island, the surface of which is soft, green, and unvaried, I do not scruple to say that, as an object of sight, it was much the more distinct. "How little faith," we exclaimed, "is due to one sense, unless its evidence be confirmed by some of its fellows! What Stranger could possibly be persuaded that this, which we know to be an unsubstantial mockery, is *really* so; and that there exists only a single Island on this beautiful Lake?" At length the appearance underwent a gradual transmutation; it lost its prominence and passed into a glimmering and dim *inversion*, and then totally disappeared;—leaving behind it a clear open area of ice of the same dimensions. We now perceived that this bed of ice, which was thinly suffused with water, had produced the illusion, by reflecting and refracting (as persons skilled in optics would no doubt easily explain) a rocky and woody section of the opposite mountain named Silver-how.

Having dwelt so much upon the beauty of pure and still water, and pointed out the advantage which the Lakes of the North of England have in this particular over those of the Alps, it would be injustice not to advert to the sublimity that must often be given to Alpine scenes, by the agitations to which those vast bodies of water are there subject. I have witnessed many tremendous thunder-storms among the Alps, and the most glorious effects of light and shadow; but I never happened to be present when any Lake was agitated by those hurricanes which I imagine must often torment them. If the commotions be at all proportionable to the expanse and depth of the waters, and the height of the surrounding mountains, then, if I may judge from what is frequently seen here, the exhibition must be awful and astonishing.—On this day, March 30, 1822, the winds have been acting upon the small Lake of Rydal, as if they had received command to carry its waters from their bed into the sky; the white billows in different quarters disappeared under clouds, or rather drifts, of spray, that were whirled along, and up into the air by scouring winds, charging each other in squadrons in every direction, upon the Lake. The spray, having been hurried aloft till it lost its consistency and whiteness, was driven along the mountain tops like flying showers that vanish in the distance. Frequently an eddying wind scooped the waters out of the basin, and forced them upwards in the very shape of an Icelandic Geyser, or boiling fountain, to the height of several hundred feet.

This small Mere of Rydal, from its position, is subject in a peculiar degree to these commotions. The present season, however, is unusually stormy;— great numbers of fish, two of them not less than 12 pounds weight, were a few days ago cast on the shores of Derwent-water by the force of the waves.

Lest, in the foregoing comparative estimate, I should be suspected of partiality to my native mountains, I will support my general opinion by the authority of Mr. West, whose Guide to the Lakes has been eminently serviceable to the Tourist for nearly 50 years. The Author, a Roman Catholic Clergyman, had passed much time abroad, and was well acquainted with the scenery of the Continent. He thus expresses himself: "They who intend to make the continental tour should begin here; as it will give, in miniature, an idea of what they are to meet with there, in traversing the Alps and Appenines; to which our northern mountains are not inferior in beauty of line, or variety of summit, number of lakes, and transparency of water; not in colouring of rock, or softness of turf; but in height and extent only. The mountains here are all accessible to the summit, and furnish prospects no less surprising, and with more variety, than the Alps themselves. The tops of the highest Alps are inaccessible, being covered with everlasting snow, which commencing at regular heights above the cultivated tracts, or wooded and verdant sides, form indeed the highest contrast in nature. For there may be seen all the variety of climate in one view. To this, however, we oppose the sight of the ocean, from the summits of all the higher mountains, as it appears intersected with promontories, decorated with islands, and animated with navigation."—West's *Guide*, p. 5.

EXCURSIONS

TO THE TOP OF SCAWFELL AND ON THE BANKS OF ULLSWATER

It was my intention, several years ago, to describe a regular tour through this country, taking the different scenes in the most favourable order; but after some progress had been made in the work it was abandoned from a conviction, that, if well executed, it would lessen the pleasure of the Traveller by anticipation, and, if the contrary, it would mislead him. The Reader may not, however, be displeased with the following extract from a letter to a Friend, giving an account of a visit to a summit of one of the highest of these mountains; of which I am reminded by the observations of Mr. West, and by reviewing what has been said of this district in comparison with the Alps.

Having left Rosthwaite in Borrowdale, on a bright morning in the first week of October, we ascended from Seathwaite to the top of the ridge, called Ash-course, and thence beheld three distinct views;—on one side, the continuous Vale of Borrowdale, Keswick, and Bassenthwaite,—with Skiddaw, Helvellyn, Saddle-back, and numerous other mountains,—and, in the distance, the Solway Frith and the Mountains of Scotland;—on the other side, and below us, the Langdale Pikes—their own vale below *them;*— Windermere,—and, far beyond Windermere, Ingleborough in Yorkshire. But how shall I speak of the deliciousness of the third prospect! At this time, *that* was most favoured by sunshine and shade. The green Vale of Esk—deep and green, with its glittering serpent stream, lay below us; and, on we looked to the Mountains near the Sea,—Black Comb pre-eminent,—and, still beyond, to the Sea itself, in dazzling brightness. Turning round we saw the Mountains of Wastdale in tumult; to our right, Great Gavel, the loftiest, a distinct, and *huge* form, though the middle of the mountain was, to our eyes, as its base.

We had attained the object of this journey; but our ambition now mounted highter. We saw the summit of Scaw-fell, apparently very near to us; and we shaped our course towards it; but, discovering that it could not be reached without first making a considerable descent, we resolved, instead, to aim at another point of the same mountain, called the *Pikes*, which I have since found has been estimated as highter than the summit bearing the name of Scawfell Head, where the Stone Man is built.

The sun had never once been overshadowed by a cloud during the whole of our progress from the centre of Borrowdale. On the summit of the Pike,

View from the Summit of Scawfell Pike, watercolour by William Turner of Oxford, 1841. 'We now beheld the whole mass of Great Gavel [Gable] from its base,—the Den of Wastdale at our feet—a gulf immeasurable; Grasmere [Grasmoor] and the other mountains of Crummock; Ennerdale and its mountains; and the Sea beyond!' An extract from Dorothy's account is inscribed on the back of the drawing. The view clearly shows Great Gable, as described in the *Guide*, as the hub of the wheel from which the lakes radiate.

which we gained after much toil, though without difficulty, there was not a breath of air to stir even the papers containing our refreshment, as they lay spread out upon a rock. The stillness seemed to be not of this world:—we paused, and kept silence to listen; and no sound could be heard: the Scawfell Cataracts were voiceless to us; and there was not an insect to hum in the air. The vales which we had seen from Ash-course lay yet in view; and, side by side with Eskdale, we now saw the sister Vale of Donnerdale terminated by the Duddon Sands. But the majesty of the mountains below, and close to us, is not to be conceived. We now beheld the whole mass of Great Gavel from its base,—the Den of Wastdale at our feet—a gulph immeasurable: Grasmire and the other mountains of Crummock—Ennerdale and its mountains; and the Sea beyond! We sat down to our repast, and gladly would we have tempered our beverage (for there was no spring or well near us) with such a supply of delicious water as we might have procured, had we been on the rival summit of Great Gavel; for on its highest point is a small triangular receptacle in the native rock, which, the shepherds say, is never dry. There we might have slaked out thirst plenteously with a pure and celestial liquid, for the cup or basin, it appears has no other feeder than the dews of heaven, the showers, the vapours, the hoar frost, and the spotless snow.

Scawfell Pikes, from Sty Head, by Thomas Allom.
The summit of Scawfell Pike is in the far distance. The pack-horses in the
foreground are crossing Sty Head Pass, the rough track which is still the only
direct link between Borrowdale and Wastdale.

While we were gazing around, "Look," I exclaimed, "at yon ship upon the glittering sea!" "Is it a ship?" replied our shepherd-guide. "It can be nothing else," interposed my companion; "I cannot be mistaken, I am so accustomed to the appearance of ships at sea." The Guide dropped the argument; but, before a minute was gone, he quietly said, "Now look at your ship; it is changed into a horse." So indeed it was,—a horse with a gallant neck and head. We laughed heartily; and, I hope, when again inclined to be positive, I may remember the ship and the horse upon the glittering sea; and the calm confidence, yet submissiveness, of our wise Man of the Mountains, who certainly had more knowledge of clouds than we, whatever might be our knowledge of ships.

I know not how long we might have remained on the summit of the Pike, without a thought of moving, had not our Guide warned us that we must not linger; for a storm was coming. We looked in vain to espy the signs of it. Mountains, vales, and sea were touched with the clear light of the sun. "It is there," said he, pointing to the sea beyond Whitehaven, and there we perceived a light vapour unnoticeable but by a shepherd accustomed to watch all mountain bodings. We gazed around again, and yet again, unwilling to lose the remembrance of what lay before us in that lofty solitude; and then prepared to depart. Meanwhile the air changed to cold, and we saw that tiny vapour swelled into mighty masses of cloud which came boiling over the mountains. Great Gavel, Helvellyn, and Skiddaw, were wrapped in storm; yet Langdale, and the mountains in that quarter, remained all bright in sunshine. Soon the storm reached us; we sheltered under a crag; and almost as rapidly as it had come it passed away, and left us free to observe the struggles of gloom and sunshine in other quarters. Langdale now had its share, and the Pikes of Langdale were decorated by two splendid rainbows. Skiddaw also had his own rainbows. Before we again reached Ash-course every cloud had vanished from every summit.

I ought to have mentioned that round the top of Scawfell-PIKE not a blade of grass is to be seen. Cushions or tufts of moss, parched and brown, appear between the huge blocks and stones that lie in heaps on all sides to a great distance, like skeletons or bones of the earth not needed at the creation, and there left to be covered with never-dying lichens, which the clouds and dews nourish; and adorn with colours of vivid and exquisite beauty. Flowers, the most brilliant feathers, and even gems, scarcely surpass in colouring some of those masses of stone, which no human eye beholds, except the shepherd or traveller be led thither by curiosity: and how seldom must this happen! For the other eminence is the one visited by the adventurous stranger; and the shepherd has no inducement to ascend the PIKE in quest of his sheep; no feed being *there* to tempt them.

We certainly were singularly favoured in the weather; for when we were seated on the summit, our conductor, turning his eyes thoughtfully round, said, "I do not know that in my whole life, I was ever, at any season of the year, so high upon the mountains on so *calm* a day." (It was the 7th of October.) Afterwards we had a spectacle of the grandeur of earth and heaven commingled; yet without terror. We knew that the storm would pass away;—for so our prophetic Guide had assured us.

Before we reached Seathwaite in Borrowdale, a few stars had appeared, and we pursued our way down the Vale, to Rosthwaite, by moonlight.

Scawfell and Helvellyn being the two Mountains of this region which will best repay the fatigue of ascending them, the following Verses may be here introduced with propriety. They are from the Author's Miscellaneous Poems.

To ——,

ON HER FIRST ASCENT TO THE SUMMIT OF HELVELLYN

INMATE of a Mountain Dwelling,
Thou hast clomb aloft, and gazed,
From the watch-towers of Helvellyn;
Awed, delighted, and amazed!

Potent was the spell that bound thee
Not unwilling to obey;
For blue Ether's arms, flung round thee,
Stilled the pantings of dismay.

Lo! the dwindled woods and meadows!
What a vast abyss is there!
Lo! the clouds, the solemn shadows,
And the glistenings—heavenly fair!

And a record of commotion
Which a thousand ridges yield;
Ridge, and gulf, and distant ocean
Gleaming like a silver shield!

—Take thy flight;—possess, inherit
Alps or Andes—they are thine!
With the morning's roseate Spirit,
Sweep their length of snowy line;

Or survey the bright dominions
In the gorgeous colours drest
Flung from off the purple pinions,
Evening spreads throughout the west!

Thine are all the coral fountains
Warbling in each sparry vault
Of the untrodden lunar mountains;
Listen to their songs!—or halt,

To Niphate's top invited,
Whither spiteful Satan steered;
Or descend where the ark alighted,
When the green earth re-appeared:

For the power of hills is on thee,
As was witnessed through thine eye
Then, when old Helvellyn won thee
To confess their majesty!

Lyulph's Tower, Gowbarrow Park, Ullswater, by Thomas Churchyard. A rare example of a picture in oils 'painted on the spot'. Lyulph's Tower, the earliest picturesque gothic revival house in the Lake District, was built by the Duke of Norfolk in 1780, as a pleasure house and hunting lodge.

Castle Cragg, Borrowdale, oil painting by J. C. Ibbetson. The artist has taken liberties with the foreground to create a romantic image of the castle-like crag which guards the Jaws of Borrowdale.

Eskdale from Muncaster Castle, watercolour by Thomas Sunderland, looking north-east up the Vale of Esk. The tower which was erected by Lord Muncaster in 1815 was on a point which terminated the castle drive.

The slopes of Ullswater
which today, as in
Wordsworth's day, are
covered in wild daffodils.

William and Mary
Wordsworth in old age,
1839, watercolour by
Margaret Gillies.

Lancaster Sands, *c.* 1826, watercolour by J. M. W. Turner. 'The Stranger . . . crossing the majestic plain
whence the sea has retired . . . beholds rising apparently from its base, the cluster of mountains among
which he is going to wander.' The traditional approach from the South to the Western Lakes,
recommended by Wordsworth, was across the sands from Lancaster, until the turnpike was completed in
1820. The crossing was hazardous and guides known as Carters were considered essential.

The Langdale Pikes from Elterwater, wash drawing
by Gainsborough. This is the only known drawing resulting from
Gainsborough's visit to the Lakes in 1783, which is topographical in character.
The others are all idealized compositions made up from Lake District elements.
It is noticeable that after 1783 sublime rocks and mountains appeared in many of
his landscapes.

Opposite above: Buttermere Lake with part of Crummock water, a shower, oil
painting by J. M. W. Turner. 'The mountains of the Vale Buttermere and
Crummock are nowhere so impressive as from the bosom of Crummock Water.'
Turner's painting was based on a sketch made in his tour of the Lakes in 1797. The
outline of the hills follows the sketch closely, but the rainbow and the boat have
been added in the studio. It was exhibited in the Academy in 1789 with a verse from
Thompson's *Seasons*: 'Til the western sky the downward sun/Looks out
effulgent—the rapid radiance instantaneous strikes/The illumin'd mountains—in a
yellow mist/Bestriding earth—the grand ethereal bow/Shoots up immense, and
every hue unfolds.'

'Rosthwaite, Borrowdale from the Road to Watenlath' by Thomas Allom.
Upper Borrowdale is one of those valleys whose bottom 'is mostly a spacious
and gently declining area, apparently laid as the floor of a temple, or the surface
of a lake' (in fact probably the site of a post-glacial lake).

Having said so much of *points of view* to which few are likely to ascend, I
am induced to subjoin an account of a short excursion through more
accessible parts of the country, made at a *time* when it is seldom seen but by
the inhabitants. As the journal was written for one acquainted with the
general features of the country, only those effects and appearances are dwelt
upon, which are produced by the changeableness of the atmosphere, or
belong to the season when the excursion was made.

A.D. 1805.—On the 7th of November, on a damp and gloomy morning, we left Grasmere Vale, intending to pass a few days on the banks of Ulswater. A mild and dry autumn had been unusually favourable to the preservation and beauty of foliage; and, far advanced as the season was, the trees on the larger Island of Rydal-mere retained a splendour which did not need the heightening of sunshine. We noticed, as we passed, that the line of the grey rocky shore of that island, shaggy with variegated bushes and shrubs, and spotted and striped with purplish brown heath, indistinguishably blending with its image reflected in the still water, produced a curious resemblance, both in form and colour, to a richly-coated caterpillar, as it might appear through a magnifying glass of extraordinary power. The mists gathered as we went along: but, when we reached the top of Kirkstone, we were glad we had not been discouraged by the apprehension of bad weather. Though not able to see a hundred yards before us, we were more than contented. At such a time, and in such a place, every scattered stone the size of one's head becomes a companion. Near the top of the Pass is the remnant of an old wall, which (magnified, though obscured, by the vapour) might have been taken for a fragment of some monument of ancient grandeur,—yet that same pile of stones we had never before even observed. This situation, it must be allowed, is not favourable to gaiety; but a pleasing hurry of spirits accompanies the surprise occasioned by objects transformed, dilated, or distorted, as they are when seen through such a medium. Many of the fragments of rock on the top and slopes of Kirkstone, and of similar places, are fantastic enough in themselves; but the full effect of such impressions can only be had in a state of weather when they are not likely to be *sought* for. It was not till we had descended considerably that the fields of Hartshope were seen, like a lake tinged by the reflection of sunny clouds: I mistook them for Brothers-water, but, soon after, we saw that Lake gleaming faintly with a steelly brightness,—then, as we continued to descend, appeared the brown oaks, and the birches of lively yellow— and the cottages—and the lowly Hall of Hartshope, with its long roof and ancient chimneys. During great part of our way to Patterdale, we had rain, or rather drizzling vapour; for there was never a drop upon our hair or clothes larger than the smallest pearls upon a lady's ring.

The following morning, incessant rain till 11 o'clock, when the sky began to clear, and we walked along the eastern shore of Ullswater towards the farm of Blowick. The wind blew strong, and drove the clouds forward, on the side of the mountain above our heads;—two storm-stiffened black yew-trees fixed our notice, seen through, or under the edge of, the flying mists,—four or five goats were bounding among the rocks;—the sheep moved about more quietly, or cowered beneath their sheltering places. This is the only part of the country where goats are now found;* but this morning, before we had seen these, I was reminded of that picturesque animal by two rams of mountain breed, both with Ammonian horns, and with beards majestic as that which Michael Angelo has given to his statue of Moses.

* A.D. 1805. These also have disappeared.

But to return; when our path had brought us to that part of the naked common which overlooks the woods and bush-besprinkled fields of Blowick, the lake, clouds, and mists were all in motion to the sound of sweeping winds;—the church and cottages of Patterdale scarcely visible, or seen only by fits between the shifting vapours. To the northward the scene was less visionary;—Place Fell steady and bold;—the whole lake driving onward like a great river—waves dancing round the small islands. The house at Blowick was the boundary of our walk; and we returned, lamenting to see a decaying and uncomfortable dwelling in a place where sublimity and beauty seemed to contend with each other. But these regrets were dispelled by a glance on the woods that clothe the opposite steeps of the lake. How exquisite was the mixture of sober and splendid hues! The general colouring of the trees was brown—rather than of ripe hazel nuts; but towards the water, there were yet beds of green, and in the highest parts of the wood, was abundance of yellow foliage, which, gleaming through a vapoury lustre, reminded us of masses of clouds, as you see them gathered together in the west, and touched with the golden light of the setting sun.

After dinner we walked up the Vale: I had never had an idea of its extent and width in passing along the public road on the other side. We followed the path that leads from house to house; two or three times it took us through some of those copses or groves that cover the little hillocks in the middle of the vale, making an intricate and pleasing intermixture of lawn and wood. Our fancies could not resist the temptation; and we fixed upon a spot for a cottage, which we began to build: and finished as easily as castles are raised in the air.—Visited the same spot in the evening. I shall say nothing of the moonlight aspect of the situation which had charmed us so much in the afternoon; but I wish you had been with us when, in returning to our friend's house, we espied his lady's large white dog, lying in the moonshine upon the round knoll under the old yew-tree in the garden, a romantic image—the dark tree and its dark shadow—and the elegant creature, as fair as a spirit! The torrents murmured softly: the mountains down which they were falling did not, to my sight furnish a back-ground for this Ossianic picture; but I had a consciousness of the depth of the seclusion, and that mountains were embracing us on all sides; "I saw not, but I *felt* that they were there."

Friday, November 9th.—Rain, as yesterday, till 10 o'clock, when we took a boat to row down the lake. The day improved,—clouds and sunny gleams on the mountains. In the large bay under Place Fell, three fishermen were dragging a net,—a picturesque group beneath the high and bare crags! A raven was seen aloft; not hovering like the kite, for that is not the habit of the bird; but passing on with a straight-forward perseverance, and timing the motion of its wings to its own croaking. The waters were agitated; and the iron tone of the raven's voice, which strikes upon the ear at all times as the more dolorous from its regularity, was in fine keeping with the wild scene before our eyes. This carniverous fowl is a great enemy to the lambs of these solitudes; I recollect frequently seeing, when a boy, bunches of unfledged ravens suspended from the churchyard gates of H——, for which a reward of *so* much a head was given to the adventurous destroyer.—The fishermen drew their net ashore, and hundreds of fish were leaping in their prison. They were all of the kind called skellies, a sort of fresh-water herring, shoals of which may sometimes be seen dimpling or rippling the surface of the lake in calm weather. This species is not found, I believe, in any other of these lakes; nor, as far as I know, is the chervin, that *spiritless* fish, (though I am loth to call it so, for it was a prime favourite with Isaac Walton,) which must frequent Ullswater, as I have seen a large shoal passing into the lake from the river Eamont. *Here* are no pike, and the char are smaller than those of the other lakes, and of inferior quality; but the grey trout attains a very large size, sometimes weighing above twenty pounds. This lordly creature seems to know that "re-tiredness is a piece of majesty;" for it is scarcely ever caught, or even seen, except when it quits the depths of the lake in the spawning season, and runs up into the streams, where it is too often destroyed in disregard of the law of the land and of nature.

Quitted the boat in the bay of Sandwyke, and pursued our way towards Martindale along a pleasant path—at first through a coppice, bordering the lake, then through green fields—and came to the village, (if village it may be called, for the houses are few, and separated from each other,) a sequestered spot, shut out from the view of the lake. Crossed the one-arched bridge, below the chapel, with its "bare ring of mossy wall," and single yew-tree. At the last house in the dale we were greeted by the master, who was sitting at his door, with a flock of sheep collected round him, for the purpose of smearing them with tar (according to the custom of the season) for protection against the winter's cold. He invited us to enter, and view a room built by Mr. Hasell for the accommodation of his friends at the annual chase of red deer in his forests at the head of these dales. The room is fitted up in the sportsman's style, with a cupboard for bottles and glasses, with strong chairs, and a dining-table; and ornamented with the horns of the stags caught at these hunts for a succession of years—the length of the last race each had run being recorded under his spreading antlers. The good woman treated us with oaten cake, new and crisp; and after this welcome refreshment and rest, we proceeded on our return to Patterdale by a short cut over the mountains. On leaving the fields of Sandwyke, while ascending by a gentle slope along the valley of Martindale, we had occasion to observe that in thinly-peopled glens of this character the general want of wood gives a peculiar interest to the scattered cottages embowered in syca-more. Towards its head, this valley splits into two parts; and in one of these (that to the left) there is no house, nor any building to be seen but a cattle-shed on the side of a hill, which is sprinkled over with trees, evidently the remains of an extensive forest. Near the entrance of the other division stands the house where we were entertained, and beyond the enclosures of that farm there are no other. A few old trees remain, relics of the forest, a little stream hastens, though with serpentine windings, through the unculti-vated hollow, where many cattle were pasturing. The cattle of this country are generally white, or light-coloured; but these were dark brown, or black, which heightened the resemblance this scene bears to many parts of the Highlands of Scotland.—While we paused to rest upon the hill-side, though

Grisedale, a valley at the head of Ullswater running up towards Helvellyn by
Thomas Allom. This is the most direct route from Grasmere to Patterdale and
was frequently traversed by the Wordsworths. In the foreground is a sled.
These were in general use in the Lake District until quite recently, for bringing
bracken down from the fells for the cattle's winter bedding.

well contented with the quiet every-day sounds—the lowing of cattle,
bleating of sheep, and the very gentle murmuring of the valley stream, we
could not but think what a grand effect the music of the bugle-horn would
have among these mountains.   It is still heard once every year, at the chase I
have spoken of; a day of festivity for the inhabitants of this district except the
poor deer, the most ancient of them all.   Our ascent even to the top was very
easy; when it was accomplished we had exceedingly fine views, some of the
lofty Fells being resplendent with sunshine, and others partly shrouded by
clouds.   Ullswater, bordered by black steeps, was of dazzling brightness;
the plain beyond Penrith smooth and bright, or rather gleamy, as the sea or
sea sands.   Looked down into Boardale, which, like Stybarrow, has been
named from the wild swine that formerly abounded here; but it has now no
sylvan covert, being smooth and bare, a long, narrow, deep, cradle-shaped
glen, lying so sheltered that one would be pleased to see it planted by human
hands, there being a sufficiency of soil; and the trees would be sheltered
almost like shrubs in a green-house.—After having walked some way along
the top of the hill, came in view of Glenriddin and the mountains at the head
of Grisdale.—Before we began to descend, turned aside to a small ruin, called
at this day the chapel, where it is said the inhabitants of Martindale and

Patterdale were accustomed to assemble for worship. There are now no traces from which you could infer for what use the building had been erected; the loose stones and the few which yet continue piled up resemble those which lie elsewhere on the mountain; but the shape of the building having been oblong, its remains differ from those of a common sheep-fold; and it has stood east and west. Scarcely did the Druids, when they fled to these fastnesses perform their rites in any situation more exposed to disturbance from the elements. One cannot pass by without being reminded that the rustic psalmody must have had the accompaniment of many a wildly-whistling blast; and what dismal storms must have often drowned the voice of the preacher! As we descend, Patterdale opens upon the eye in grand simplicity, screened by mountains, and proceeding from two heads, Deepdale and Hartshope, where lies the little lake of Brotherswater, named in old maps Broaderwater, and probably rightly so; for Bassenthwaite-mere at this day, is familiarly called Broadwater; but the change in the appellation of this small lake or pool (if it be a corruption) may have been assisted by some melancholy accident similar to what happened about twenty years ago, when two brothers were drowned there, having gone out to take their holiday pleasure upon the ice on a new-year's day.

A rough and precipitous peat track brought us down to our friend's house.—Another fine moonlight night; but a thick fog rising from the neighbouring river, enveloped the rocky and wood-crested knoll on which our fancy-cottage had been erected; and, under the damp cast upon my feelings, I consoled myself with moralising on the folly of hasty decisions in matters of importance, and the necessity of having at least one year's knowledge of a place before you realise airy suggestions in solid stone.

Saturday, November 10th. At the breakfast-table tidings reached us of the death of Lord Nelson, and of the victory at Trafalgar. Sequestered as we were from the sympathy of a crowd, we were shocked to hear that the bells had been ringing joyously at Penrith to celebrate the triumph. In the rebellion of the year 1745, people fled with their valuables from the open country to Patterdale, as a place of refuge secure from the incursions of strangers. At that time, news such as we had heard might have been long in penetrating so far into the recesses of the mountains; but now, as you know, the approach is easy, and the communication, in summer time, almost hourly: nor is this strange, for travellers after pleasure are become not less active, and more numerous than those who formerly left their homes for purposes of gain. The priest on the banks of the remotest stream of Lapland will talk familiarly of Buonaparte's last conquests, and discuss the progress of the French revolution, having acquired much of his information from adventurers impelled by curiosity alone.

The morning was clear and cheerful after a night of sharp frost. At 10 o'clock we took our way on foot towards Pooley Bridge, on the same side of the lake we had coasted in a boat the day before.—Looked backwards to the south from our favourite station above Blowick. The dazzling sunbeams striking upon the church and village, while the earth was steaming with exhaltations not traceable in other quarters, rendered their forms even more indistinct than the partial and flitting veil of unillumined vapour had done

171

two days before.   The grass on which we trod, and the trees in every thicket were dripping with melted hoar-frost.   We observed the lemon-coloured leaves of the birches, as the breeze turned them to the sun, sparkle, or rather *flash*, like diamonds, and the leafless purple twigs were tipped with globes of shining crystal.

The day continued delightful, and unclouded to the end.   I will not describe the country which we slowly travelled through, nor relate our adventures: and will only add, that on the afternoon of the 13th we returned along the banks of Ullswater by the usual road.   The lake lay in deep repose after the agitations of a wet and stormy morning.   The trees in Gowbarrow park were in that state when what is gained by the disclosure of their bark and branches compensates, almost, for the loss of foliage, exhibiting the variety which characterises the point of time between autumn and winter.   The hawthorns were leafless; their round heads covered with rich green berries, and adorned with arches of green brambles, and eglantines hung with glossy hips; and the grey trunks of some of the ancient oaks, which in the summer season might have been regarded only for their venerable majesty, now attracted notice by a pretty embellishment of green mosses and fern intermixed with russet leaves retained by those slender outstarting twigs which the veteran tree would not have tolerated in his strength.   The smooth silver branches of the ashes were bare; most of the alders as green as the Devonshire cottage-myrtle that weathers the snows of Christmas.—Will

Brothers' Water and Deepdale by J. B. Pyne.
Dorothy describes how, on their return from the 'Excursion on the Banks of Ullswater', 'The steeps were reflected in Brothers-water, and, above the lake, appeared like enormous black perpendicular walls.'

Kirkstone Pass by T. H. Fielding. Wordsworth makes his ode, 'The Pass of Kirkstone', the conclusion of the *Guide*.

you accept it as some apology for my having dwelt so long on the woodland ornaments of these scenes—that artists speak of the trees on the banks of Ullswater, and especially along the bays of Stybarrow crags, as having a peculiar character of picturesque intricacy in their stems and branches, which their rocky stations and the mountain winds have combined to give them.

At the end of Gowbarrow park a large herd of deer were either moving slowly or standing still among the fern. I was sorry when a chance-companion, who had joined us by the way, startled them with a whistle, disturbing an image of grave simplicity and thoughtful enjoyment; for I could have fancied that those natives of this wild and beautiful region were partaking with us a sensation of the solemnity of the closing day. The sun had been set some time; and we could perceive that the light was fading away from the coves of Helvellyn, but the lake under a luminous sky, was more brilliant than before.

After tea at Patterdale, set out again:—a fine evening; the seven stars close to the mountain-top; all the stars seemed brighter than usual. The steeps were reflected in Brotherswater, and, above the lake, appeared like enormous black perpendicular walls. The Kirkstone torrents had been swoln by the rains, and now filled the mountain pass with their roaring, which added greatly to the solemnity of our walk. Behind us, when we had climbed to a great height, we saw one light, very distinct, in the vale, like a large red star— a solitary one in the gloomy region. The cheerfulness of the scene was in the sky above us.

Reached home a little before midnight. The following verses (from the Author's Miscellaneous Poems,) after what has just been read may be acceptable to the reader, by way of conclusion to this little Volume.

ODE

THE PASS OF KIRKSTONE

1.

WITHIN the mind strong fancies work,
A deep delight the bosom thrills,
Oft as I pass along the fork
Of these fraternal hills:
Where, save the rugged road, we find
No appanage of human kind;
Nor hint of man, if stone or rock
Seem not his handy-work to mock
By something cognizably shaped;
Mockery—or model roughly hewn,
And left as if by earthquake strewn:
Or from the Flood escaped:
Altars for Druid service fit;
(But where no fire was ever lit,
Unless the glow-worm to the skies
Thence offer nightly sacrifice;)
Wrinkled Egyptian monument;
Green moss-grown tower; or hoary tent;
Tents of a camp that never shall be razed;
On which four thousand years have gazed!

2.

Ye plough-shares sparkling on the slopes!
Ye snow-white lambs that trip
Imprisoned 'mid the formal props
Of restless ownership!
Ye trees, that may to-morrow fall
To feed the insatiate Prodigal!
Lawns, houses, chattels, groves, and fields,
All that the fertile valley shields;
Wages of folly—baits of crime,—
Of life's uneasy game the stake,
Playthings that keep the eyes awake
Of drowsy, dotard Time;
O care! O guilt!—O vales and plains,
Here, 'mid his own unvexed domains,
A Genius dwells, that can subdue
At once all memory of You,—
Most potent when mists veil the sky,
Mists that distort and magnify;
While the course rushes, to the sweeping breeze,
Sigh forth their ancient melodies!

174

3.

List to those shriller notes!—*that* march
Perchance was on the blast,
When through this Height's inverted arch,
Rome's earliest legion passed!
—They saw, adventurously impelled,
And older eyes than theirs beheld,
This block—and yon, whose Church-like frame
Gives to the savage Pass its name.
Aspiring Road! that lov'st to hide
Thy daring in a vapoury bourn,
Not seldom may the hour return
When thou shalt be my Guide:
And I (as often we find cause,
When life is at a weary pause,
And we have panted up the hill
Of duty with reluctant will)
Be thankful, even though tired and faint,
For the rich bounties of Constraint;
Whence oft invigorating transports flow
That Choice lacked courage to bestow!

4.

My Soul was grateful for delight
That wore a threatening brow;
A veil is lifted—can she slight
The scene that opens now?
Though habitation none appear,
The greenness tells, man must be there;
The shelter—that the perspective
Is of the clime in which we live;
Where Toil pursues his daily round;
Where Pity sheds sweet tears, and Love,
In woodbine bower or birchen grove,
Inflicts his tender wound.
—Who comes not hither ne'er shall know
How beautiful the world below;
Nor can he guess how lightly leaps
The brook adown the rocky steeps.
Farewell, thou desolate Domain!
Hope, pointing to the cultured Plain,
Carols like a shepherd boy;
And who is she?—Can that be Joy!
Who, with a sun-beam for her guide,
Smoothly skims the meadows wide;
While Faith, from yonder opening cloud,
To hill and vale proclaims aloud,
"Whate'er the weak may dread, the wicked dare,
Thy lot, O man, is good, thy portion fair!"

ITINERARY

The Publishers, with permission of the Author,
have added the following
ITINERARY OF THE LAKES,
FOR THE USE OF TOURISTS.

STAGES.	Miles
Lancaster to Kendal, by Kirkby Lonsdale,	30
Lancaster to Kendal, by Burton,	22
Lancaster to Kendal, by Milnthorpe,	21
Lancaster to Ulverston, over Sands,	21
Lancaster to Ulverston, by Levens Bridge,	35½
Ulverston to Hawkshead, by Coniston Water Head,	19
Ulverston to Bowness, by Newby Bridge,	17
Hawkshead to Ambleside,	5
Hawkshead to Bowness,	6
Kendal to Ambleside,	14
Kendal to Ambleside, by Bowness,	15
From and back to Ambleside round the two Langdales,	18
Ambleside to Ullswater,	10
Ambleside to Keswick,	16¼
Keswick to Borrowdale, and round the Lake,	12
Keswick to Borrowdale and Buttermere,	23
Keswick to Wastdale and Calder Bridge,	27
Calder Bridge to Buttermere and Keswick,	29
Keswick, round Bassenthwaite Lake,	18
Keswick to Patterdale, Pooley Bridge, and Penrith,	38
Keswick to Pooley Bridge and Penrith,	24
Keswick to Penrith,	17½
Whitehaven to Keswick,	27
Workington to Keswick,	21
Excursion from Penrith to Hawes Water,	27
Carlisle to Penrith,	18
Penrith to Kendal,	26

Inns and Public Houses, when not mentioned, are marked thus.*

LANCASTER to KENDAL, by KIRKBY LONSDALE, 30 m.

Miles.		Miles.	Miles.		Miles.
5	Caton	5	2	Tunstall	13
2	Claughton	7	2	Burrow	15
2	Hornby*	9	2	Kirkby Lonsdale. ..	17
2	Melling	11	13	Kendal .. .,. ..	30

INNS.—*Lancaster*, King's Arms, Commercial Inn, Royal Oak.
INNS.—*Kirkby Lonsdale*, Rose and Crown, Green Dragon.

LANCASTER to KENDAL, by BURTON, 21¾ m.

10¾	Burton	10¾	½	End Moor*	16
4¾	Crooklands*	15½	5¾	Kendal	21¾

INNS.—*Kendal*, King's Arms, Commercial Inn.—*Burton*, Royal Oak, King's Arms.

LANCASTER to KENDAL, by MILNTHORPE, 21¼ m.

2¾	Slyne*	2¾	4	Hale*	12
1¼	Bolton-le-Sands* ..	4	½	Beethom*	12½
2	Carnforth*	6	1¼	Milnthorpe	13¾
2	Junction of the		1¼	Heversham*	15
	Milnthorp and ..	8	1½	Levens-bridge	16½
	Burton roads		4¾	Kendal	21¼

INN.—*Milnthorpe*, Cross Keys.

LANCASTER to ULVERSTON, over SANDS, 21 m.

3½	Hest Bank*	3½	1¼	Flookburgh*	15
¼	Lancaster Sands ..	3¾	¾	Cark	15¾
9	Kent's Bank	12¾	¼	Leven Sands	16
1	Lower Allithwaite ..	13¾	5	Ulverston	21

INNS.—*Ulverston*, Sun Inn, Bradyll's Arms.

LANCASTER to ULVERSTON, by LEVENS BRIDGE, 35½ m.

12	Hale*	12	3	Lindal*	23½
½	Beethom*	12½	2	Newton*	25½
1¼	Milnthorp	13¾	2	Newby-Bridge* ..	27½
1¼	Heversham*	15	2	Low Wood	29½
2¾	Levens-bridge	16½	3	Greenodd	32½
4	Witherslack*	20½	3	Ulverston	35½

ULVERSTON to HAWKSHEAD, by CONISTON WATER-HEAD, 19 m.

6	Lowick-bridge	6	8	Coniston Water-Head*	16
2	Nibthwaite	8	3	Hawkshead	19

INN.—*Hawkshead*, Red Lion.

ULVERSTON to BOWNESS, by NEWBY-BRIDGE, 16 m.

3	Green Odd	3	2	Newby-bridge	8
3	Low Wood	6	8	Bowness	16

INNS.—*Bowness*, White Lion, Crown Inn.

HAWKSHEAD to AMBLESIDE, 5 m.

HAWKSHEAD to BOWNESS, 5½ m.

2	Sawrey	2	1½	Bowness	5½
2	Windermere-ferry* ..	4			

KENDAL to AMBLESIDE, 13½ m.

5	Staveley*	5	1½	Troutbeck-bridge* ..	10
1½	Ings Chapel	6½	2	Low Wood Inn	12
2	Orrest-head	8½	1½	Ambleside	13½

INNS.—*Ambleside*, Salutation Hotel, Commercial Inn.

KENDAL to AMBLESIDE, by BOWNESS, 15 m.

4	Crook*	4	2½	Troutbeck-bridge ..	11½
2	Gilpin Bridge*	6	2	Low Wood Inn	13½
3	Bowness	9	1½	Ambleside	15

A CIRCUIT from and back to AMBLESIDE by LITTLE and GREAT LANGDALE, 18 m.

3	Skelwith-bridge* ..	3	2	Langdale Chapel Stile*	13
2	Colwith Cascade ..	5	5	By High Close and	
3	Blea Tarn	8		Rydal to Ambleside..	18
3	Dungeon Ghyll.. ..	11			

AMBLESIDE to ULLSWATER, 10 m.

4	Top of Kirkstone ..	4	3	Inn at Patterdale ..	10
3	Kirkstone Foot	7			

AMBLESIDE to KESWICK, 16¼ m.

1½	Rydal	1½	4	Smalthwaite-bridge ..	12¼
3½	Swan, Grassmere* ..	5	3	Castlerigg	15¼
2	Dunmail Raise	7	1	Keswick	16¼
1¼	Nag's Head, Wythburn	8¼			

EXCURSIONS FROM KESWICK.

INNS.—*Keswick*, Royal Oak, Queen's Head.

To BORROWDALE, and ROUND THE LAKE, 12 m.

2	Barrow-house	2	1	Return to Grange ..	6
1	Lowdore	3	4½	Portinscale..	10½
1	Grange	4	1½	Keswick	12
1	Bowder Stone	5			

To BORROWDALE and BUTTERMERE.

5	Bowder Stone	..	..	5	4	Gatesgarth..	12
1	Rosthwaite..	..	..	6	2	Buttermere*	14
2	Seatoller	..	..	8	9	Keswick, by Newlands	23

TWO DAYS' EXCURSION TO WASTDALE, ENNERDALE, and LOWES-WATER.

FIRST DAY.

6	Rosthwaite..	..	..	6	6	Strands,* Nether	
2	Seatoller	..	..	8		Wastdale	20
1	Seathwaite..	..	..	9	4	Gosforth*	24
3	Sty-head	..	..	12	3	Calder Bridge*	27
2	Wastdale-head	..	..	14			

SECOND DAY.

7	Ennerdale Bridge	..	7	3	Scale-hill*	16
3	Lamplugh Cross*	..	10	4	Buttermere*	20
4	Lowes Water	..	14	9	Keswick	29

KESWICK ROUND BASSENTHWAITE WATER.

8	Peel Wyke* .	..	..	8	3	Bassenthwaite	
1	Ouse Bridge	..	..	9		Sand-bed	13
1	Castle Inn ..	..	..	10	5	Keswick	18

KESWICK to PATTERDALE, and by POOLEY BRIDGE to PENRITH.

10	Springfield*	..	..	10	10	Pooley Bridge* through	
7	Gowbarrow Park	..	17		Gowbarrow Park ..	32
5	Patterdale*..	..	..	22	6	Penrith	38

INNS.—*Penrith*, Crown Inn, The George.

KESWICK to POOLEY BRIDGE and PENRITH.

12	Penruddock*	..	..	12	3	Pooley Bridge	18
3	Dacre*	..	..	15	6	Penrith	24

KESWICK to PENRITH, 17½ m.

4	Threlkeld*..	..	..	4	3½	Stainton*	15
7½	Penruddock	..	..	11½	2½	Penrith	17½

WHITEHAVEN to KESWICK, 27 m.

2	Moresby	..	..	2	5	Cockermouth	14
2	Distington..	..	..	4	2½	Embleton	16½
2	Winscales ..	..	..	6	6½	Thornthwaite	23
3	Little Clifton	..	..	9	4	Keswick	27

INNS.—*Whitehaven*, Black Lion, Golden Lion, the Globe.
INNS.—*Cockermouth*, The Globe, The Sun.

WORKINGTON to KESWICK, 21 m.

The road joins that from Whitehaven to Keswick 4 miles from Workington.
INNS.—*Workington*, Green Dragon, New Crown, King's Arms.

EXCURSION from PENRITH to HAWESWATER.

5	Lowther, or Askham*	5		5	Over Moor Dovack to Pooley	21
7	By Bampton* to Hawes Water	12		6	By Dalemain to Penrith	27
4	Return by Butterswick	16				

CARLISLE to PENRITH, 18 m.

2½	Carlton*	2½		2	Plumpton*	13
7	Low Hesket*	9½		5	Penrith	18
1½	High Hesket*	11				

INNS.—*Carlisle*, The Bush, Coffee House, King's Arms.

PENRITH to KENDAL, 26 m.

1	Eamont Bridge*	1		6¾	Hawse Foot*	17
1½	Clifton*	2½		4	Plough Inn*	21
2	Hackthorpe*	4½		2½	Skelsmergh Stocks*	23½
5¾	Shap	10¼		2½	Kendal	26

INN.—*Shap*, Greyhound, King's Arms.

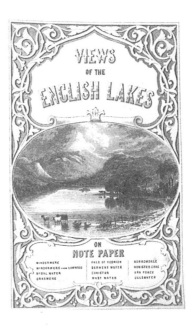

A packet of Lake District note paper. Engravings of Lake District views, such as those from drawings by Thomas Allom, were used as headings for note paper, sold in the District. This envelope contained twelve sheets of paper with a different view on each. Paper of this sort was being used by the Wordsworth circle in the 1840s, and continued to be on sale until the end of the century.

Left: The heron by Edward Lear. 'The stately heron may be descried with folded wings, that might seem to have caught their delicate hue from the blue waters, the side of which she watches for her sustenance.' This is one of the splendid plates in John Gould's *Birds of Europe* from drawings by Edward Lear, who made an extensive sketching tour in the Lakes in 1836. The birds were a feature of the Lake District which made a significant appeal to Wordsworth.

Right: The Gorge of Wathenlath with the falls of Lodore, watercolour by Thomas Girtin, 1801. Girtin visited the Lakes in 1801 and probably also in 1800. The Cataract of Lodore, which made such a strong appeal to most visitors and inspired Southey's well-known jingle 'How does the water come down at Lodore', seems to have had no particular appeal for Wordsworth.

Ullswater from the foot of Gowbarrow Fell, oil painting by J. C. Ibbetson. Ibbetson settled at Ambleside in 1800 and lived there and later at Troutbeck for about five years. He was befriended by Sir George and Lady Beaumont. He painted many versions of this much painted prospect of Ullswater.

View of the Lake District, watercolour by Peter de Wint. De Wint seems to have stayed with the Lonsdales at Lowther Castle, and most of his Lake District views, like this one of the mountains at the head of Ullswater, are of scenes among the eastern fells, generally seen over broad moorland foregrounds. He is known to have met Wordsworth who sent him a message of thanks and regard in 1840.

Tent Lodge, Coniston, watercolour by J. M. W. Turner, 1818. Tent Lodge was so called because Elizabeth Smith spent much of the year preceding her death from consumption in 1806 reclining in a tent pitched here 'on a knoll on the sloping bank of Conistone Water', where, according to a eulogy by Wordsworth on the talented young poetess, whom he never met, 'the sufferer answered that if she could not be well with such a heavenly sight before her, she could be well no where'. Tent Lodge was built after her death.

The two waterfalls at Rydal, watercolours by Francis Towne. *Right*: Upper Cascade. *Far right*: Lower Cascade. These two cascades, close together in the Rydal Beck and close to Rydal Mount were two of the most popular sites for tourists and artists in search of the picturesque. A garden house was built in the grounds of Rydal Hall from which the prospect of the Lower Cascade and the bridge above it could be viewed, framed in a window.

Patterdale in 1797, watercolour by J. M. W. Turner. The old church, 'an edifice . . . scarcely larger than many of the single stones and fragments of rock which are scattered near it', was pulled down soon after Turner's visit to make place for a new church.

William Wordsworth. Oil painting by Benjamin Robert Haydon, 1842. 'A picture by Mr Haydon, representing me in the act of climbing Helvellyn.' He had made the ascent of Helvellyn in 1840, at the age of seventy. Elizabeth Barrett Browning was inspired by Haydon's portrait to write a sonnet, 'Wordsworth upon Helvellyn', which she sent to him with a copy of her poems.

Raven Crag, watercolour by Francis Towne. This is a leaf from a sketch-book, inscribed on the back 'Light from the left hand 12 o'clock Raven Cragg with part of Thirlmere Lake in the Vale of St. John in Cumberland. Drawn by Francis Towne August 17th 1786'. Towne was fascinated by the structure of the mountains and recorded their anatomy with delicate outline in brown ink washed over with cool translucent watercolour. The Wordsworths frequently passed close to Raven Crag on their way to and from Keswick.

APPENDIX

KENDAL AND WINDERMERE RAILWAY
TWO LETTERS
RE-PRINTED FROM THE MORNING POST
REVISED, WITH ADDITIONS

KENDAL:
PRINTED BY R. BRANTHWAITE AND SON
[1844]

SONNET ON THE PROJECTED KENDAL AND WINDERMERE RAILWAY

Is then no nook of English ground secure
From rash assault? Schemes of retirement sown
In youth, and 'mid the busy world kept pure
As when their earliest flowers of hope were blown,
Must perish;—how can they this blight endure?
And must he too the ruthless change bemoan
Who scorns a false utilitarian lure
'Mid his paternal fields at random thrown?
Baffle the threat, bright Scene, from Orrest-head
Given to the pausing traveller's rapturous glance:
Plead for thy peace, thou beautiful romance
Of nature; and, if human hearts be dead,
Speak, passing winds; ye torrents, with your strong
And constant voice, protest against the wrong.

WILLIAM WORDSWORTH.

RYDAL MOUNT,
    October 12th, 1844.

The degree and kind of attachment which many of the yeomanry feel to their small inheritances can scarcely be overrated. Near the house of one of them stands a magnificent tree, which a neighbour of the owner advised him to fell for profit's sake. 'Fell it,' exclaimed the yeoman, 'I had rather fall on my knees and worship it.' It happens, I believe, that the intended railway would pass through this little property, and I hope that an apology for the answer will not be thought necessary by one who enters into the strength of the feeling. W. W.

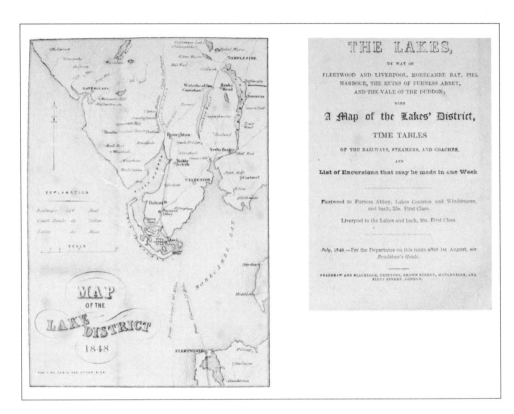

Bradshaw's Railway and Steamer timetables for the Lake District, combined
with a brief guide and a map, published July 1848, in the year after the opening
of the Kendal and Windermere Railway. Round trips could be made from
Liverpool, Fleetwood and Southport to Ambleside, by ship, coach and train. On
the steamer 'Helvellyn' passengers were entertained by Herr Schmidt and his
band.

KENDAL AND WINDERMERE RAILWAY

No. I.

To the Editor of the *Morning Post*.

Sɪʀ—

Some little time ago you did me the favour of inserting a sonnet expressive of the regret and indignation which, in common with others all over these Islands, I felt at the proposal of a railway to extend from Kendal to Low Wood, near the head of Windermere. The project was so offensive to a large majority of the proprietors through whose lands the line, after it came in view of the lake, was to pass, that, for this reason, and the avowed one of the heavy expense without which the difficulties in the way could not be overcome, it has been partially abandoned, and the terminus is now announced to be at a spot within a mile of Bowness. But as no guarantee can be given that the project will not hereafter be revived, and an attempt made to carry the line forward through the vales of Ambleside and Grasmere, and as in one main particular the case remains essentially the same, allow me to address you upon certain points which merit more consideration than the favourers of the scheme have yet given them. The matter, though seemingly local, is really one in which all persons of taste must be interested, and, therefore, I hope to be excused if I venture to treat it at some length.

I shall barely touch upon the statistics of the question, leaving these to the two adverse parties, who will lay their several statements before the Board of Trade, which may possibly be induced to refer the matter to the House of Commons; and, contemplating that possibility, I hope that the observations I have to make may not be altogether without influence upon the public, and upon individuals whose duty it may be to decide in their place whether the proposed measure shall be referred to a Committee of the House. Were the case before us an ordinary one, I should reject such an attempt as presumptuous and futile; but it is not only different from all others, but, in truth, peculiar.

In this district the manufactures are trifling; mines it has none, and its quarries are either wrought out or superseded; the soil is light, and the cultivateable parts of the country are very limited; so that it has little to send out, and little has it also to receive. Summer Tourists (and the very word precludes the notion of a railway) it has in abundance; but the inhabitants are so few and their intercourse with other places so infrequent, that one daily coach, which could not be kept going but through its connection with the Post-office, suffices for three-fourths of the year along the line of country as far as Keswick. The staple of the district is, in fact, its beauty and its character of seclusion and retirement; and to these topics and to others connected with them my remarks shall be confined.

The projectors have induced many to favour their schemes by declaring that one of their main objects is to place the beauties of the Lake district within easier reach of those who cannot afford to pay for ordinary conveyances. Look at the facts. Railways are completed, which, joined with others in rapid progress, will bring travellers who prefer approaching by Ullswater to within four miles of that lake.

The Lancaster and Carlisle Railway will approach the town of Kendal, about eight or nine miles from eminences that command the whole vale of Windermere. The lakes are therefore at present of very easy access for *all* persons; but if they be not made still more so, the poor, it is said, will be wronged. Before this be admitted let the question be fairly looked into, and its different bearings examined. No one can assert that, if this intended mode of approach be not effected, anything will be taken away that is actually possessed. The wrong, if any, must lie in the unwarrantable obstruction of an attainable benefit. First, then, let us consider the probable amount of that benefit.

Elaborate gardens, with topiary works, were in high request, even among our remote ancestors, but the relish for choice and picturesque natural *scenery* (a poor and mean word which requires an apology, but will be generally understood) is quite of recent origin. Our earlier travellers—Ray, the naturalist, one of the first men of his age—Bishop Burnet, and others who had crossed the Alps, or lived some time in Switzerland, are silent upon the sublimity and beauty of those regions; and Burnet even uses these words, speaking of the Grisons—"When they have made up estates elsewhere they are glad to leave Italy and the best parts of Germany, and to come and live among those mountains of which the very sight is enough to fill a man with horror." The accomplished Evelyn, giving an account of his journey from Italy through the Alps, dilates upon the terrible, the melancholy, and the uncomfortable; but, till he comes to the fruitful country in the neighbourhood of Geneva, not a syllable of delight or praise. In the *Sacra Telluris Theoria* of the other Burnet there is a passage—omitted, however, in his own English translation of the work—in which he gives utterance to his sensations, when, from a particular spot he beheld a tract of the Alps rising before him on the one hand, and on the other the Mediterranean Sea spread beneath him. Nothing can be worthier of the magnificent appearances he describes than his language. In a noble strain also does the Poet Gray address, in a Latin Ode, the *Religio loci* at the Grande Chartruise. But before his time, with the exception of the passage from Thomas Burnet just alluded to, there is not, I believe, a single English traveller whose published writings would disprove the assertion, that, where precipitous rocks and mountains are mentioned at all, they are spoken of as objects of dislike and fear, and not of admiration. Even Gray himself, describing, in his Journal, the steeps at the entrance of Borrowdale, expresses his terror in the language of Dante:—"Let us not speak of them, but look and pass on." In my youth, I lived some time in the vale of Keswick, under the roof of a shrewd and sensible woman, who more than once exclaimed in my hearing, "Bless me! folk are always talking about prospects: when I was young there was never sic a thing neamed.' In fact, our ancestors, as everywhere appears, in choosing the site of their houses, looked only at shelter and convenience, especially of water, and often would place a barn or any other out-house directly in front of their habitations, however beautiful the landscape which their windows might otherwise have commanded. The first house that was built in the Lake district for the sake of the beauty of the country was the work of a Mr. English, who had travelled in Italy, and chose for his site, some eighty years ago, the great island of Windermere; but it was sold before his building was finished, and he showed how little he was capable of appreciating the character of the situation by setting up a length of high garden-wall, as exclusive as it was ugly, almost close to the house. The nuisance was swept away when the late Mr. Curwen became the owner of this favoured spot. Mr. English was followed by Mr. Pocklington, a native of Nottinghamshire, who played strange pranks by his buildings and plantations upon Vicar's Island, in Derwentwater, which his admiration, such as it was, of the country, and probably a wish to be a leader in a new fashion, had tempted him to purchase. But what has all this to do with the subject?—Why, to show that a vivid perception of romantic scenery is neither inherent in mankind, nor a necessary consequence of even a comprehensive

Pocklington's Island and the Vale of Newlands by John 'Warwick' Smith in 1795,
showing The House, The Battery, St Mary's Church and The Boat House.

education. It is benignly ordained that green fields, clear blue skies, running
streams of pure water, rich groves and woods, orchards, and all the ordinary varieties
of rural nature, should find an easy way to the affections of all men, and more or less
so from early childhood till the senses are impaired by old age and the sources of mere
earthly enjoyment have in a great measure failed. But a taste beyond this, however
desirable it may be that every one should possess it, is not to be implanted at once; it
must be gradually developed both in nations and individuals. Rocks and mountains, torrents and wide-spread waters, and all those features of nature which go to
the composition of such scenes as this part of England is distinguished for, cannot, in
their finer relations to the human mind, be comprehended, or even very imperfectly
conceived, without processes of culture or opportunities of observation in some
degree habitual. In the eye of thousands and tens of thousands, a rich meadow,
with fat cattle grazing upon it, or the sight of what they would call a heavy crop of
corn, is worth all that the Alps and Pyrenees in their utmost grandeur and beauty
could show to them; and, notwithstanding the grateful influence, as we have
observed, of ordinary nature and the productions of the fields, it is noticeable. what
trifling conventional prepossessions will, in common minds, not only preclude
pleasure from the sight of natural beauty, but will even turn it into an object of
disgust. "If I had to do with this garden," said a respectable person, one of my
neighbours, "I would sweep away all the black and dirty stuff from that wall." The

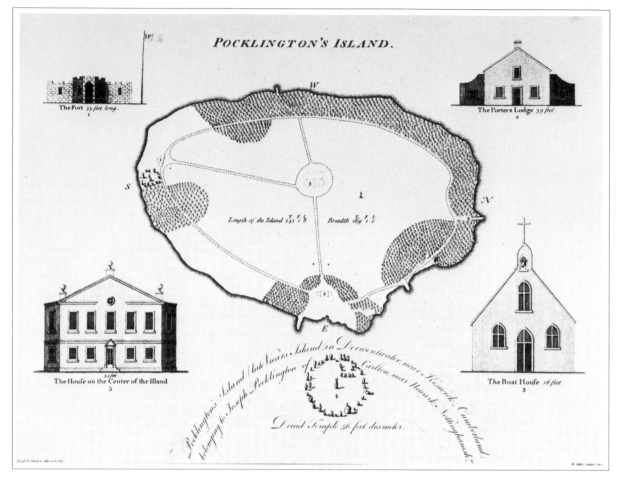

POCKLINGTON'S ISLAND.

The Fort *33 feet long.*
1

The Porters Lodge *39 feet.*
2

The House on the Center of the Island
5

The Boat House *16 feet*
3

Length of the Island 251 7/8 *Broadth* 169 1/10

Druid Temple 56 feet diameter.

Pocklington's Island (late Vicars Island) in Derwentwater near Keswick, Cumberland belonging to Joseph Pocklington of Carlton near Newark, Nottinghamshire.

Crosthwaite's plan of Pocklington's Island
in Derwentwater. Mr Pocklington, an eccentric gentleman from Nottinghamshire
'played strange pranks by his buildings and plantations upon Vicar's Island, . . .,
which his admiration, such as it was, of the country and probably a wish to be a
leader in a new fashion, had tempted him to purchase'. Among the follies shown
on the plan is a Druid Temple (no. 4), built from stones excavated for the
foundations of the house (no. 5). On another plan Pocklington describes it as
'discovered on y.ᵉ 3.ᵈ Day of Sep.ʳ in the Year 1779 . . . supposed to be the most
compleat & last built Temple in Europe'.

wall was backed by a bank of earth, and was exquisitely decorated with ivy, flowers,
moss, and ferns, such as grow of themselves in like places; but the mere notion of
fitness associated with a trim garden-wall prevented, in this instance, all sense of the
spontaneous bounty and delicate care of nature.   In the midst of a small pleasure-
ground, immediately below my house, rises a detached rock, equally remarkable for
the beauty of its form, the ancient oaks that grow out of it, and the flowers and shrubs
which adorn it.   "What a nice place would this be," said a Manchester tradesman,
pointing to the rock, "if that ugly lump were but out of the way."   Men as little

advanced in the pleasure which such objects give to others are so far from being rare, that they may be said fairly to represent a large majority of mankind. This is a fact, and none but the deceiver and the willingly deceived can be offended by its being stated. But as a more susceptible taste is undoubtedly a great acquisition, and has been spreading among us for some years, the question is, what means are most likely to be beneficial in extending its operation? Surely that good is not to be obtained by transferring at once uneducated persons in large bodies to particular spots, where the combinations of natural objects are such as would afford the greatest pleasure to those who have been in the habit of observing and studying the peculiar character of such scenes, and how they differ one from another. Instead of tempting artisans and labourers, and the humbler classes of shopkeepers, to ramble to a distance, let us rather look with lively sympathy upon persons in that condition, when, upon a holiday, or on the Sunday, after having attended divine worship, they make little excursions with their wives and children among neighbouring fields, whither the whole of each family might stroll, or be conveyed at much less cost than would be required to take a single individual of the number to the shores of Windermere by the cheapest conveyance. It is in some such way as this only, that persons who must labour daily with their hands for bread in large towns, or are subject to confinement through the week, can be trained to a profitable intercourse with nature where she is the most distinguished by the majesty and sublimity of her forms.

For further illustration of the subject, turn to what we know of a man of extraordinary genius, who was bred to hard labour in agricultural employments, Burns, the poet. When he had become distinguished by the publication of a volume of verses, and was enabled to travel by the profit his poems brought him, he made a tour, in the course of which, as his companion, Dr. Adair, tells us, he visited scenes inferior to none in Scotland in beauty, sublimity, and romantic interest; and the Doctor having noticed, with other companions, that he seemed little moved upon one occasion by the sight of such a scene, says—"I doubt if he had much taste for the picturesque." The personal testimony, however, upon this point is conflicting; but when Dr. Currie refers to certain local poems as decisive proofs that Burns' fellow-traveller was mistaken, the biographer is surely unfortunate. How vague and tame are the poet's expressions in those few local poems, compared with his language when he is describing objects with which his position in life allowed him to be familiar! It appears, both from what his works contain, and from what is not to be found in them, that, sensitive as they abundantly prove his mind to have been in its intercourse with common rural images, and with the general powers of nature, exhibited in storm and in stillness, in light or darkness, and in the various aspects of the seasons, he was little affected by the sight of one spot in preference to another, unless where it derived an interest from history, tradition, or local associations. He lived many years in Nithsdale, where he was in daily sight of Skiddaw, yet he never crossed the Solway for a better acquaintance with that mountain; and I am persuaded that, if he had been induced to ramble among our lakes, by that time sufficiently celebrated, he would have seldom been more excited than by some ordinary Scottish stream or hill with a tradition attached to it, or which had been the scene of a favourite ballad or love song. If all this be truly said of such a man, and the like cannot be denied of the eminent individuals before named, who to great natural talents added the accomplishments of scholarship or science, then what ground is there for maintaining that the poor are treated with disrespect, or wrong done to them or any class of visitants, if we be reluctant to introduce a railway into this country for the sake of lessening, by eight or nine miles only, the fatigue or expense of their journey to Windermere?—And wherever any one among the labouring classes has made even an approach to the sensibility which drew a lamentation from Burns when he had uprooted a daisy with his plough, and caused him to turn the "weeder-clips aside" from the thistle, and spare "the symbol dear" of his country, then surely such a one, could he afford by any means to travel as far as Kendal, would not grudge a two hours' walk across the skirts of the beautiful country that he was desirous of visiting.

The wide-spread waters of these regions are in their nature peaceful; so are the steep mountains and the rocky glens; nor can they be profitably enjoyed but by a mind disposed to peace. Go to a pantomime, a farce, or a puppet-show, if you want noisy pleasure—the crowd of spectators who partake your enjoyment will, by their presence and acclamations, enhance it; but may those who have given proof that they prefer other gratifications continue to be safe from the molestation of cheap trains pouring out their hundreds at a time along the margin of Windermere; nor let any one be liable to the charge of being selfishly disregardful of the poor, and their innocent and salutary enjoyments, if he does not congratulate himself upon the especial benefit which would thus be conferred on such a concourse.

> O, Nature, a' thy shows an' forms,
> To feeling pensive hearts hae charms!

So exclaimed the Ayrshire ploughman, speaking of ordinary rural nature under the varying influences of the seasons, and the sentiment has found an echo in the bosoms of thousands in as humble a condition as he himself was when he gave vent to it. But then they were feeling, pensive hearts; men who would be among the first to lament the facility with which they had approached this region, by a sacrifice of so much of its quiet and beauty, as, from the intrusion of a railway, would be inseparable. What can, in truth, be more absurd than that either rich or poor should be spared the trouble of travelling by the high roads over so short a space, according to their respective means, if the unavoidable consequence must be a great disturbance of the retirement, and in many places a destruction of the beauty of the country, which the parties are come in search of? Would not this be pretty much like the child's cutting up his drum to learn where the sound came from?

Having, I trust, given sufficient reason for the belief that the imperfectly educated classes are not likely to draw much good from rare visits to the lakes performed in this way, and surely on their own account it is not desirable that the visits should be frequent, let us glance at the mischief which such facilities would certainly produce. The directors of railway companies are always ready to devise or encourage entertainments for tempting the humbler classes to leave their homes. Accordingly, for the profit of the shareholders and that of the lower class of inn-keepers, we should have wrestling matches, horse and boat races without number, and pot-houses and beer-shops would keep pace with these excitements and recreations, most of which might too easily be had elsewhere. The injury which would thus be done to morals, both among this influx of strangers and the lower class of inhabitants, is obvious; and, supposing such extraordinary temptations not to be held out, there cannot be a doubt that the Sabbath day in the towns of Bowness and Ambleside, and other parts of the district, would be subject to much additional desecration.

Whatever comes of the scheme which we have endeavoured to discountenance, the charge against its opponents of being selfishly regardless of the poor, ought to cease. The cry has been raised and kept up by three classes of persons—they who wish to bring into discredit all such as stand in the way of their gains or gambling speculations; they who are dazzled by the application of physical science to the useful arts, and indiscriminately applaud what they call the spirit of the age as manifested in this way; and, lastly, those persons who are ever ready to step forward in what appears to them to be the cause of the poor, but not always with becoming attention to particulars. I am well aware that upon the first class what has been said will be of no avail, but upon the two latter some impression will, I trust, be made.

To conclude. The railway power, we know well, will not admit of being materially counteracted by sentiment; and who would wish it where large towns are connected, and the interests of trade and agriculture are substantially promoted, by such mode of intercommunication? But be it remembered, that this case is, as has been said before, a peculiar one, and that the staple of the country is its beauty and its character of retirement. Let then the beauty be undisfigured and the retirement unviolated, unless there be reason for believing that rights and interests of a higher kind and more apparent than those which have been urged in behalf of the projected intrusion will compensate the sacrifice. Thanking you for the judicious observations that have appeared in your paper upon the subject of railways,

I remain, Sir,
Your obliged,
WM. WORDSWORTH.

Rydal Mount, Dec. 9, 1844.

NOTE.—To the instances named in this letter of the indifference even of men of genius to the sublime forms of nature in mountainous districts, the author of the interesting Essays, in the Morning Post, entitled Table Talk, has justly added Goldsmith, and I give the passage in his own words.

"The simple and gentle-hearted Goldsmith, who had an exquisite sense of rural beauty in the familiar forms of hill and dale, and meadows with their hawthorn-scented hedges, does not seem to have dreamt of any such thing as beauty in the Swiss Alps, though he traversed them on foot, and had therefore the best opportunities of observing them. In his poem "The Traveller," he describes the Swiss as loving their mountain homes, not by reason of the romantic beauty of the situation, but in spite of the miserable character of the soil, and the stormy horrors of their mountain steeps—

> Turn we to survey
> Where rougher climes a nobler race display,
> Where the bleak Swiss their stormy mansion tread,
> And force a churlish soil for scanty bread.
> No produce here the barren hills afford,
> But man and steel, the soldier and his sword:
> No vernal blooms their torpid rocks array,
> But winter lingering chills the lap of May;
> No Zephyr fondly sues the mountain's breast,
> But meteors glare and stormy glooms invest.
> Yet still, *even here*, content can spread a charm,
> Redress the clime, and all its rage disarm.'

In the same Essay (December 18th, 1844) are many observations judiciously bearing upon the true character of this and similar projects.

No. II.

To the Editor of the *Morning Post*.

SIR,

As you obligingly found space in your journal for observations of mine upon the intended Kendal and Windermere Railway, I venture to send you some further remarks upon the same subject. The scope of the main argument, it will be recollected, was to prove that the perception of what has acquired the name of picturesque and romantic scenery is so far from being intuitive, that it can be produced only by a slow and gradual process of culture; and to show, as a consequence, that the humbler ranks of society are not, and cannot be, in a state to gain material benefit from a more speedy access than they now have to this beautiful region. Some of our opponents dissent from this latter proposition, though the most judicious of them readily admit the former; but then, overlooking not only positive assertions, but reasons carefully given, they say, "As you allow that a more comprehensive taste is desirable, you ought to side with us''; and they illustrate their position, by reference to the British Museum and National Picture Gallery. ''There,'' they add, ''thanks to the easy entrance now granted, numbers are seen, indicating by their dress and appearance their humble condition, who, when admitted for the first time, stare vacantly around them, so that one is inclined to ask what brought them hither? But an impression is made, something gained which may induce them to repeat the visit until light breaks in upon them, and they take an intelligent interest in what they behold.'' Persons who talk thus forget that, to produce such an improvement, frequent access at small cost of time and labour is indispensable. Manchester lies, perhaps, within eight hours' railway distance of London; but surely no one would advise that Manchester operatives should contract a habit of running to and fro between that town and London, for the sake of forming an intimacy with the British Museum and National Gallery? No, no; little would all but a very few gain from the opportunities which, consistently with common sense, could be afforded them for such expeditions. Nor would it fare better with them in respect of trips to the Lake district; an assertion, the truth of which no one can doubt, who has learned by experience how many men of the same or higher rank, living from their birth in this very region, are indifferent to those objects around them in which a cultivated taste takes so much pleasure. I should not have detained the reader so long upon this point, had I not heard (glad tidings for the directors and traffickers in shares!) that among the affluent and benevolent manufacturers of Yorkshire and Lancashire are some who already entertain the thought of sending, at their own expense, large bodies of their workmen, by railway, to the banks of Windermere. Surely those gentlemen will think a little more before they put such a scheme into practice. The rich man cannot benefit the poor, nor the superior the inferior, by anything that degrades him. Packing off men after this fashion, for holiday entertainment, is, in fact, treating them like children. They go at the will of their master, and must return at the same, or they will be dealt with as transgressors.

A poor man, speaking of his son, whose time of service in the army was expired, once said to me (the reader will be startled at the expression, and I, indeed, was greatly shocked by it), ''I am glad he has done with that *mean* way of life.'' But I soon gathered what was at the bottom of the feeling. The father overlooked all the glory that attaches to the character of a British soldier, in the consciousness that his son's will must have been in so great a degree subject to that of others. The poor man felt where the true dignity of his species lay, namely, in a just proportion between actions governed by a man's own inclinations and those of other men; but, according to the father's notion, that proportion did not exist in the course of life from which his son had been released. Had the old man known from experience the degree of liberty allowed to the common soldier, and the moral effect of the obedience required, he would have thought differently, and had he been capable of extending his views, he would have felt how much of the best and noblest part of our civic spirit was owing to our military and naval institutions, and that perhaps our very existence as a free people had by them been maintained. This extreme instance has been adduced to show how deeply seated in the minds of Englishmen is their sense of personal independence. Master-manufacturers ought never to lose sight of this truth. Let them consent to a Ten Hours' Bill, with little or, if possible, no diminution of wages, and the necessaries of life being more easily procured, the mind will develope itself accordingly, and each individual would be more at liberty to make at his own cost excursions in any direction which might be most inviting to him. There would then be no need for their masters sending them in droves scores of miles from their homes and families to the borders of Windermere, or anywhere else. Consider also the state of the Lake district; and look, in the first place, at the little town of Bowness, in the event of such railway inundations. What would become of it in this, not the Retreat, but the Advance, of the Ten

Thousand? Leeds, I am told, has sent as many at once to Scarborough. We should have the whole of Lancashire, and no small part of Yorkshire, pouring in upon us to meet the men of Durham, and the borderers from Cumberland and Northumberland. Alas, alas, if the lakes are to pay this penalty for their own attractions!

—Vane could tell what ills from beauty spring,
And Sedley cursed the form that pleased a king.

The fear of adding to the length of my last long letter prevented me from entering into details upon private and personal feelings among the residents, who have cause to lament the threatened intrusion. These are not matters to be brought before a Board of Trade, though I trust there will always be of that board members who know well that as we do "not live by bread alone," so neither do we live by political economy alone. Of the present board I would gladly believe there is not one who, if his duty allowed it, would not be influenced by considerations of what may be felt by a gallant officer now serving on the coast of South America, when he shall learn that the nuisance, though not intended actually to enter his property, will send its omnibuses, as fast as they can drive, within a few yards of his modest abode, which he built upon a small domain purchased at a price greatly enhanced by the privacy and beauty of the situation. Professor Wilson (him I take the liberty to name), though a native of Scotland, and familiar with the grandeur of his own country, could not resist the temptation of settling long ago among our mountains. The place which his public duties have compelled him to quit as a residence, and may compel him to part with, is probably dearer to him than any spot upon earth. The reader should be informed with what respect he has been treated. Engineer agents, to his astonishment, came and intruded with their measuring instruments, upon his garden. He saw them; and who will not admire the patience that kept his hands from their shoulders? I must stop.

But with the fear before me of the line being carried, at a day not distant, through the whole breadth of the district, I could dwell, with much concern for other residents, upon the condition which they would be in if that outrage should be committed; nor ought it to be deemed impertinent were I to recommend this point to the especial regard of Members of Parliament who may have to decide upon the question. The two Houses of Legislature have frequently shown themselves not unmindful of private feeling in these matters. They have, in some cases, been induced to spare parks and pleasure grounds. But along the great railway lines these are of rare occurrence. They are but a part, and a small part; here it is far otherwise. Among the ancient inheritances of the yeomen, surely worthy of high respect, are interspersed through the entire district villas, most of them with such small domains attached that the occupants would be hardly less annoyed by a railway passing through their neighbour's ground than through their own. And it would be unpardonable not to advert to the effect of this measure on the interests of the very poor in this locality. With the town of Bowness I have no *minute* acquaintance; but of Ambleside, Grasmere, and the neighbourhood, I can testify from long experience, that they have been favoured by the residence of a gentry whose love of retirement has been a blessing to these vales; for their families have ministered, and still minister, to the temporal and spiritual necessities of the poor, and have personally superintended the education of the children in a degree which does those benefactors the highest honour, and which is, I trust, gratefully acknowledged in the hearts of all whom they have relieved, employed, and taught. Many of those friends of our poor would quit this country if the apprehended change were realized, and would be succeeded by strangers not linked to the neighbourhood, but flitting to and fro between their fancy-villas and the homes where their wealth was accumulated and accumulating by trade and manufactures. It is obvious that persons, so unsettled, whatever might be their good wishes and readiness to part with money for charitable purposes, would ill supply the loss of the inhabitants who had been driven away.

It will be felt by those who think with me upon this occasion that I have been writing on behalf of a social condition which no one who is competent to judge of it will be willing to subvert, and that I have been endeavouring to support moral sentiments and intellectual pleasures of a high order against an enmity which seems growing more and more formidable every day; I mean "Utilitarianism," serving as a mask for cupidity and gambling speculations. My business with this evil lies in its reckless mode of action by Railways, now its favourite instruments. Upon good authority I have been told that there was lately an intention of driving one of these pests, as they are likely too often to prove, through a part of the magnificent ruins of Furness Abbey—an outrage which was prevented by some one pointing out how easily a deviation might be made; and the hint produced its due effect upon the engineer.

Sacred as that relic of the devotion of our ancestors deserves to be kept, there are temples of Nature, temples built by the Almighty, which have a still higher claim to be left unviolated. Almost every reach of the winding vales in this district might once have presented itself to a man of imagination and feeling under that aspect, or as the Vale of Grasmere appeared to the Poet Gray more than seventy years ago. "No flaring gentleman's-house," says he, "nor garden-walls break in upon the repose of this little unsuspected *paradise*, but all is peace," &c., &c. Were the Poet now living, how would he have lamented the probable intrusion of a railway with its scarifications, its intersections, its noisy machinery, its smoke, and swarms of pleasure-hunters, most of them thinking that they do not fly fast enough through the country which they have come to see. Even a broad highway may in some places greatly impair the characteristic beauty of the country, as will be readily acknowledged by those who remember what the Lake of Grasmere was before the new road that runs along its eastern margin had been constructed.

> Quanto praestantius esset
> Numen aquae viridi si margine clauderet undas
> Herba—

As it once was, and fringed with wood, instead of the breastwork of bare wall that now confines it. In the same manner has the beauty, and still more the sublimity of many Passes in the Alps been injuriously affected. Will the reader excuse a quotation from a MS. poem in which I attempted to describe the impression made upon my mind by the descent towards Italy along the Simplon before the new military road had taken the place of the old muleteer track with its primitive simplicities?

> Brook and road
> Were fellow-travellers in this gloomy pass,
> And with them did we journey several hours
> At a slow step. The immeasurable height
> Of woods decaying, never to be decayed,
> The stationary blasts of waterfalls,
> And in the narrow rent, at every turn,
> Winds thwarting winds bewildered and forlorn,
> The torrents shooting from the clear blue sky,
> The rocks that muttered close upon our ears,
> Black drizzling crags that spake by the way-side
> As if a voice were in them, the sick sight
> And giddy prospect of the raving stream,
> The unfettered clouds and region of the heavens,
> Tumult and peace, the darkness and the light,

Were all like workings of one mind, the features
Of the same face, blossoms upon one tree,
Characters of the great Apocalypse,
The types and symbols of Eternity,
Of first, and last, and midst, and without end.

1799.

Thirty years afterwards I crossed the Alps by the same Pass: and what had become of the forms and powers to which I had been indebted for those emotions? Many of them remained of course undestroyed and indestructible. But, though the road and torrent continued to run parallel to each other, their fellowship was put an end to. The stream had dwindled into comparative insignificance, so much had Art interfered with and taken the lead of Nature; and although the utility of the new work, as facilitating the intercourse of great nations, was readily acquiesced in, and the workmanship, in some places, could not but excite admiration, it was impossible to suppress regret for what had vanished for ever. The oratories heretofore not infrequently met with, on a road still somewhat perilous, were gone; the simple and rude bridges swept away; and instead of travellers proceeding, with leisure to observe and feel, were pilgrims of fashion hurried along in their carriages, not a few of them perhaps discussing the merits of "the last new Novel," or poring over their Guide-books, or fast asleep. Similar remarks might be applied to the mountainous country of Wales; but there too, the plea of utility, especially as expediting the communication between England and Ireland, more than justifies the labours of the Engineer. Not so would it be with the Lake District. A railroad is already planned along the sea coast, and another from Lancaster to Carlisle is in great forwardness: an intermediate one is therefore, to say the least of it, superfluous. Once for all let me declare that it is not against Railways but against the abuse of them that I am contending.

How far I am from undervaluing the benefit to be expected from railways in their legitimate application will appear from the following lines published in 1837, and composed some years earlier.

STEAMBOATS AND RAILWAYS.

Motions and Means, on sea on land at war
With old poetic feeling, not for this
Shall ye, by poets even, be judged amiss!
Nor shall your presence, howsoe'er it mar
The loveliness of nature, prove a bar
To the mind's gaining that prophetic sense
Of future good, that point of vision, whence
May be discovered what in soul ye are;
In spite of all that Beauty must disown
In your harsh features, nature doth embrace
Her lawful offspring in man's Art; and Time,
Pleased with your triumphs o'er his brother Space,
Accepts from your bold hand the proffered crown
Of hope, and welcomes you with cheer sublime.

I have now done with the subject. The time of life at which I have arrived may, I trust, if nothing else will, guard me from the imputation of having written from any selfish interests, or from fear of disturbance which a railway might cause to myself. If gratitude for what repose and quiet in a district hitherto, for the most part, not disfigured but beautified by human hands, have done for me through the course of a long life, and hope that others might hereafter be benefited in the same manner and in the same country, be selfishness, then, indeed, but not otherwise, I plead guilty to the charge.   Nor have I opposed this undertaking on account of the inhabitants of the district *merely*, but, as hath been intimated, for the sake of every one, however humble his condition, who coming hither shall bring with him an eye to perceive, and a heart to feel and worthily enjoy.   And as for holiday pastimes, if a scene is to be chosen suitable to them for persons thronging from a distance, it may be found elsewhere at less cost of every kind.   But, in fact, we have too much hurrying about in these islands; much for idle pleasure, and more from over activity in the pursuit of wealth, without regard to the good or happiness of others.

Proud were ye, Mountains, when, in times of old,
Your patriot sons, to stem invasive war,
Intrenched your brows; ye gloried in each scar:
Now, for your shame, a Power, the Thirst of Gold,
That rules o'er Britain like a baneful star,
Wills that your peace, your beauty, shall be sold,
And clear way made for her triumphal car
Through the beloved retreats your arms enfold!
Heard YE that Whistle?   As her long-linked Train
Swept onwards, did the vision cross your view?
Yes, ye were startled;—and, in balance true,
Weighing the mischief with the promised gain,
Mountains, and Vales, and Floods, I call on you
To share the passion of a just disdain.
WILLIAM WORDSWORTH.

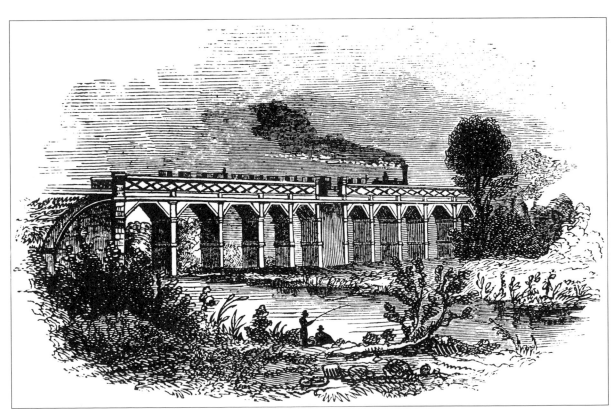

Viaduct on the Kendal and Windermere Railway in 1847.
A print published the year the railway was opened.

Chronology

A Chronology of events related to Wordsworth and the Lake District

1770 7 April. WILLIAM WORDSWORTH born at Cockermouth.

1771 25 December. Dorothy Wordsworth born.

1772 4 December. John Wordsworth born. Coleridge born.
William Gilpin tours Lakes.

1774 9 June. Christopher Wordsworth born. Southey born.
Thomas Gray's *Journal* of 1769 first published.

1776 During 1776–7 WW and Mary Hutchinson attend Anne Birkett's infant
school at Penrith.

1777 Farington with Sir George Beaumont in Lakes.

1778 Mother dies. West's *Guide* first published.

1779 WW attends Hawkshead Grammar School. Lodges with Ann Tyson.

1783 Father dies. Gainsborough and de Loutherbourg in Lakes.

1786 *Dear Native Regions.*
Francis Towne in Lakes. Gilpin's *Observations* published.

1787 Enters St John's College, Cambridge.

1789 Long vacation with Dorothy Wordsworth and Mary Hutchinson at Penrith.
Evening Walk finished. Farington's *Views of the Lakes* published, letter press
by WW's uncle Wm. Cookson.

1793 *Evening Walk* published.

1794 Visits to Lake District.

1795 Visits Penrith. Meets Coleridge and Southey.
October, settles at Racedown with Dorothy.

1797 July, moves to Alfoxden.
Turner tours Lakes.

1798 At Alfoxden until June. *Lyrical Ballads* first published.

1799 October, walking tour in Lakes with Coleridge and John Wordsworth.
20 December, settles at Dove Cottage, Grasmere, with Dorothy.

1800 June–July, Coleridge at Dove Cottage. August, Coleridge with wife and
Hartley settles at Greta Hall, Keswick. January–September, John Wordsworth
at Dove Cottage. Mary Hutchinson visits Dove Cottage twice.

1802 4 October, marries Mary Hutchinson.
Coleridge's solitary walking tour.

1803 18 June, birth of John. The Southeys join the Coleridges at Greta Hall. Sir George Beaumont presents WW with small estate at Applethwaite. John Harden settles at Brathay Hall.

1804 16 August, birth of Dora. Coleridge goes to Malta.

1805 5 February, John Wordsworth lost at sea.
WW ascends Helvellyn with Walter Scott and Humphry Davy.
Excursion to Ullswater with Dorothy.
The Prelude finished.

1806 16 June, birth of Thomas.
Spends winter at Coleorton with the Beaumonts, visited by Coleridge.
September–October, Constable in Lakes.

1807 4 November, De Quincey visits Dove Cottage.

1808 June, moves from Dove Cottage to Allan Bank.
6 September, birth of Catharine.
Coleridge and De Quincey at Allan Bank.

1809 De Quincey settles at Dove Cottage.

1810 12 May, birth of William.
Select Views published.
Quarrel with Coleridge.

1811 May, moves from Allan Bank to Rectory.

1812 Deaths of Catharine and Thomas.

1813 Appointed Distributor of Stamps for Westmorland.
1 May, moves from Rectory to Rydal Mount.

1814 Tour in Scotland with Mary and Sara Hutchinson.
The Excursion published.

1818 7 October, Dorothy's excursion to the summit of Scawfell Pike.

1820 *River Duddon Sonnets*.
Westall's *Views of the Lake and Vale of Keswick* (letter press by Southey).

1822 First separate edition of the *Guide*.

1823 Fourth edition of the *Guide*.

1827 Death of Sir George Beaumont.

1832 Rose's *Westmorland, Cumberland . . . Illustrated*.

1834 Death of Coleridge.

1835 Death of Sara Hutchinson.
Dorothy's mental breakdown.
Fifth edition of the *Guide*.

1840 WW ascends Helvellyn.

1841 11 May, Dora marries Edward Quillinan.

1842 Hudson's *Complete Guide*.
WW resigns Distributorship of Stamps.

1843 Appointed Poet Laureate on death of Southey. Second edition of Hudson's *Complete Guide*.

1844 September, tour through the Duddon Valley with the Quillinans and Lady Richardson.

1845 Kendal and Windermere Railway letters republished.
Harriet Martineau comes to Ambleside.

1846 Third Edition of Hudson's *Complete Guide*.

1847 Death of Dora.
Kendal and Windermere Railway opened.

1850 23 April, WILLIAM WORDSWORTH died.
The Prelude ; or, Growth of a Poet's Mind published.

List of Illustrations

Bibliography

Editions of Wordsworth's *Guide to the Lakes* published during his lifetime.

1a *Select Views in Cumberland, Westmoreland, and Lancashire.* By the Rev. Joseph Wilkinson, Rector of East and West Wretham, in the county of Norfolk, and Chaplain to the Marquis of Huntly. London: published for the Rev. Joseph Wilkinson, by R. Ackermann, at his Repository of Arts, 101, Strand. 1810. Folio.

Issued in twelve monthly parts. 'Harrison and Rutter, printers' on title; 'William Savage, printers' on covers. Forty-eight soft-ground etchings by W. F. Wells from drawings by Wilkinson. Anonymous 'Introduction', 'Section I' and 'Section II' (by Wordsworth). In some copies the plates are coloured.

1b The letter press and the plates were reissued with a new title page. Title as before except imprint: 'London: Ackermann. 1817. S. Mills printers, Thetford.' In a copy of this issue in the Alpine Club Library, London, the plates are tinted with a yellow monochrome wash.

1c The letter press was reprinted and reissued with the plates. Title as before except imprint: 'London: Ackermann. 1821. Printed by C. Lloyd, Thetford.'

Plates issued coloured and uncoloured.

There are no changes in the text. This can be considered the true third edition of Wordsworth's *Guide* (second edition no. 2 below, 1820).

2 *The River Duddon, a Series of Sonnets : Vaudracour & Julia : and Other Poems.* To which is annexed, a Topographical Description of the Country of the Lakes, in the North of England. By William Wordsworth. London: printed for Longman, Hurst, Rees, Orme, and Brown, Paternoster-Row, 1820. Octavo.

The Introduction and the Sections from *Select Views* were rewritten 'with emendations and additions'. All references to Wilkinson's views were removed, the whole was converted into one continuous essay, and several descriptive passages and comments were added.

3 *A Description of the Scenery of the Lakes in the North of England.* Third Edition, (now first published separately) With Additions, and Illustrative Remarks upon the Scenery of the Alps. By William Wordsworth. London: printed for Longman, Hurst, Rees, Orme, and Brown, Paternoster-Row. 1822. Duodecimo.

The book was divided into three main parts: 'Description of the Scenery of the Lakes', 'Miscellaneous Observations' and 'Directions and Information for the Tourist', and included a folding map. Among the additions was an unacknowledged version of Dorothy Wordsworth's account of her excursion up Scawfell Pike, October 7, 1818.

500 copies were printed.

4   Title as no. 3 (above) except 'Fourth Edition' for 'Third Edition' and '1823' for '1822'. Text printed by A. and R. Spottiswoode, New-Street-Square. Map as before. Duodecimo.

There were many alterations and additions, including descriptions of waterfowl and of night scenes, and a new Division, 'Excursions to the Top of Scawfell and on the Banks of Ullswater', in which Dorothy's account of the excursion of November 1805, is added to her Scawfell account.

1000 copies were printed.

5   *A Guide through the District of the Lakes in the North of England, with a Description of the Scenery, &c. for the use of Tourists and Residents*. Fifth Edition, with considerable additions. By William Wordsworth. Kendal: published by Hudson and Nicholson, and in London by Longman & Co., Moxon, and Whittaker & Co. 1835. Map as before. Small octavo.

The book was rearranged with, 'Directions and information for the Tourist', 'Description of the Scenery of the Lakes' (in three Sections), 'Miscellaneous Observations', 'Excursions', 'Ode: The Pass of Kirkstone' and added by the Publishers, with permission of the Author, 'Itinerary of the Lakes'.

1500 copies were printed.

6   *A Complete Guide to the Lakes, Comprising Minute Directions for the Tourist, with Mr. Wordsworth's Description of the Scenery of the Country, &c. And Three Letters on the Geology of the Lake District*. By the Rev. Professor Sedgwick. Edited by the Publishers. Kendal: published by Hudson and Nicholson. London: Longman and Co., and Whittaker and Co. Liverpool: Webb, Castle St., Manchester: Simm and Co. 1842. Map, frontispiece and four outlines of mountains. Duodecimo.

Eight plates (four engravings, three outlines of mountains, one geological section), plan, map.

Two more editions were published during Wordsworth's lifetime in 1843 and 1845. Three more were published subsequently in 1853, 1859 and 1864.

The differences between the texts of the five original editions of the *Guide* are dealt with in detail in *The Prose Works of William Wordsworth*. Edited by W. J. B. Owen and Jane Worthington Smyser, Oxford, 1974. Vol. 2.

Index